The Hidden Power of the Heart

"*The Hidden Power of the Heart* is a beacon to those who really want to transform their own lives. Graduates of HeartMath will hold in their hands the potential for positive change that could reverberate world-wide. This book should be required reading."
— *Vernon H. Mark, M.D., Director Emeritus of Boston City Hospital, author of* Brain Power

"*The Hidden Power of the Heart* is a beautifully written book. I highly recommend it to anyone seeking more love and peace in their lives."
— *R. Jennifer Barr, Director of Development World Business Academy*

"*The Hidden Power of the Heart* joins the ranks of superior books designed to help all people."
— *Friend's Review*

"I have been in the ministry for 17 years and I have never found a process so dynamic and life transforming as is laid out in *The Hidden Power of the Heart!*"
— *Jim Peterson, Unity Church Minister*

"This is not only a heart-warming book, but a heart-winning book as well."
— *Roy Rowan, author of* The Intuitive Manager

A Planetary Publications Release

in cooperation with

THE INSTITUTE OF HEARTMATH

The Hidden Power of the Heart

Achieving Balance and Fulfillment in a Stressful World

Sara Paddison

 Planetary Publications

Published in the United States of America by:

Planetary Publications

P.O. Box 66, Boulder Creek, California 95006

(800) 372-3100 (408) 338-2161

Manufactured in the United States of America by Baker-Johnson

First printing September 1992

Cover Design by Sandy Royall

Excerpts reprinted from *Vibrational Medicine* by Richard Gerber, M.D., Copyright 1988 Bear & Co., P.O. Drawer 2860, Santa Fe, NM 87504

Library of Congress Cataloging In Publication Data

Paddison, Sara

The hidden power of the heart : achieving balance and fulfillment in a stressful world / by Sara Paddison.

p. cm.

ISBN 1-879052-17-2

1. Stress (Psychology)- -Prevention. 2. Self-realization (Psychology)
I. Title.

BF575.S75P235 1992

158'.1 - - dc20   92-32852

CIP

10 9 8 7 6 5 4 3 2 1

TABLE OF CONTENTS

AUTHOR'S PREFACE

The Institute of HeartMath, of which I am Vice President, is a nonprofit educational and research organization founded by Doc Lew Childre. Drawing upon the diverse educational, professional and cultural backgrounds of the Institute's staff and associates — which include the fields of business, education, psychology, physics, math, communication, music, and art — the Institute has developed and practiced a system of energy-efficiency and self-empowerment called HeartMath™. Much of what I will share with you in this book I discovered while working and growing side-by-side with friends at the Institute. They are extremely dedicated and loving people.

The Institute's mission is to reduce stress in the world by helping people develop greater self-management, self-esteem and self-empowerment through a deeper understanding of "heart intelligence." As the Doc says, "This system is designed to dissipate stress on contact rather than allow it to accumulate. And it works if you work with it. It doesn't take long to get results." More than forty people working at the Institute have proven out this system of self-empowerment before offering it to others. Thank you, Doc, for providing a step-by-step, nuts and bolts method of energy-efficiency in the human system that shows how the Heart Empowerment of YOU — mentally, emotionally and physically — accelerates human evolution.

Wouldn't the next template for World Understanding be something that could touch the hearts of the people? *The Hidden Power of the Heart* is a story of how I went from inner rags to riches and how my life appreciated in value. I went from 90% okay days and 10% good days to 10% good days and 90% great days. Your heart intelligence activates magnetics that serve you and teach you how to experience deeper levels of love, care and understanding of people. You make contact with your own heart power within. It's a system of you and yourself.

There is such a magnificent energy or force deep inside people. It is my hope that each and everyone concerned has a chance to experience their real heart power—or at least get a chance to experience love, so that you have a fair honest choice to love or not to love. Uncovering this hidden power is a personal process of understanding how it works and understanding yourself. You can do it because anyone can.

Thank you, Debbie Rozman, Bruce Cryer, and Wendy Rickert, the editors from the Institute of HeartMath, and others like Dick Freed, Joseph Sundram, Robert Massy, Ph.D., and Tom Beckman who were involved in the final creation of this book. Thank you for your experiences and examples I used. Hopefully, a practical understanding of the "common sense" of the heart can add to the quality of people's lives in this stressful world. Thanks to Sandy Royall, our artist in residence who did the cover design. Thank you to my parents for bringing me into this world and being responsible for me until I knew how. Thank you to my two sisters for being my friends growing up. Thank you to my former husband, Al Paddison, a co-worker at the Institute who went through my early years of growth with me. Thank you, Christian, for adding a sparkle to my life. And thanks to everyone in life with whom I have shared a moment in time. All of you have become part of my holographic reality.

Earlier in my life I was lonely, withdrawn, frightened of my own shadow. Once, while in college, I tried to commit suicide. I was confused, as so many young people are today. But I was a survivor in life, always knowing there was an answer somewhere. I grew up on military bases and my family was always moving from one base to another. Each move was like a different movie that I had to jump into. I'd be one place and be real popular. Then we'd move to another place and the kids at school were so different I'd be really shy and keep to myself. Trying to be accepted was a big deal to me. I had to keep readjusting to a lot of changes in life. I kept wondering why was life like this? What was I doing here? In art school, I found peace and family. I loved art, but the people were even more important to me. I graduated from East Carolina University with a Bachelor of Fine Arts degree and also took many courses in psychology. I came to realize that life is about caring for people. That became my ambition. My real credentials for writing this book are that I practiced and practiced truly loving and caring.

Like many people who grew up in the '60s, I was affected by the spirit of that whole decade. When President Kennedy was shot, I remember exactly where I was in the school yard and the looks on everyone's faces. Time seemed to have stopped as the entire nation went into shock. The love that people had for him was an eye-opener for me. I remembered the words he is most famous for, "Ask not what your country can do for you, ask what you can do for your country." The idealism and openness of the '60s gave my generation a surge of hope. A seed was planted that has been dormant since then. Now in the '90s, I see that our dreams weren't idealistic. They just needed time to mature. People are beginning to reawaken to what they glimpsed then: that love and care for people is what it's all about. Having been brought up in the military, I was always acutely aware that they are the caretakers of America. I appreciate the discipline, dedication and service they give our country.

As pollster George H. Gallup Jr., says, "I've always wanted to see surveys that probe beneath the surface of life." His surveys show that, "The deeper one goes, the more open one becomes." Thank you, Doc, for your love and care, for facilitating my inner awakening, for helping me understand the people business and for being a true friend in learning how to balance it all. And deep thanks to God, for this incredible Divine Plan you are unfolding for all humanity.

My universal self would like to say thank you in the way Ken Carey did in his book *Vision*. Thank you to: "Holy Mother, Truth: all matter is her body, the Earth is her eye." Thank you to: "Holy Father, Love: the stars are his flesh, Spirit is his I." I did wake up in a wonderful reality to my surprise — as one creating my reality with God.

Sara Paddison

Chapter 1

The Hidden Power of the Heart

What is the "hidden power of the heart"? A magnificent energy or force? Deep inside, people hope there is a hidden power like that — a power that could change their lives. But, to many in this stressful world, the idea of a hidden power is remote, like a faraway dream from another time. To others it seems like an unrealistic fantasy. Nevertheless, the possibility is intriguing. Why? People have an intuitive sense, like a homing device or inner antenna, that's curious about the possibility of a hidden power.

About sixteen years ago, my heart stirred. I'd just finished college and felt a yearning for a deeper understanding of life — like a core feeling in the center of my chest. But it didn't seem to be physical. I knew it was my heart. "But what is this heart I'm feeling?" I asked myself. It was a kaleidoscope of feelings: hope and despair, love and fear, swirling around within my heart.

It felt like the center of my being. I wanted to understand what my heart was saying to me, "What is this heart that can stir me? What is the human heart really?"

These questions started me on a journey that has brought much fulfillment and wonder into my life. I've experienced an awesome adventure that's taken me into the deep recesses of my heart and opened doors I never knew existed. I discovered the hidden power within my own heart. If this sounds like a faraway dream or fairy tale, I understand. That's how I might have thought about it before my journey began.

In the languages of the world, there are countless references to the feelings of the heart. Over the years, I came to realize these feelings contain within them a power to seek, to understand, to do. Step by step in this book, you and I will unravel an understanding of this untapped source of energy in you, me and every individual. We will look at its implications for the entire human race.

Heart power is simply *the electricity of your inner strength and potential*. It's what gives you the self-motivated ability to manifest and complete your goals — to *empower* yourself and *achieve balance and fulfillment* even in today's increasingly stressful world. Uncovering this hidden power is a personal process of understanding how it works and understanding yourself.

HOW POWER WORKS

To me, the word "power" means a source of energy and a capacity for action. I see it as both a faculty — like the power of thinking — and as spirit. To many, power can be frightening — like someone or something having control over you.

Let's take the example of money as power. Money is a potent form of energy that seems to have a controlling influence of its own. If someone unexpectedly handed me a thousand dollars, that money would have the power to give me a feeling of elation at that moment. If it were a million dollars, I would experience a tremendous feeling and a greater sense of power. The power that money brings really comes from a person's identification with both a feeling and a perception associated with the "frequency band" of energy called money.

So what's a frequency band? A frequency is an electromagnetic wave, a line of energy that has its own rate of vibration or oscillation. Most people know Einstein discovered the mathematical equation and fundamental law of physics, $E = mc^2$, which proved that *all things* in the universe are forms of energy that move or vibrate on their own wavelengths. Einstein's simple scientific insights have had a profound impact on the world. They have given us television, satellite communication and the atomic bomb. They gave us electron microscopes, lasers, the microwave and many other conveniences. Our physical lives changed dramatically because of this discovery. What about our mental and emotional lives? Are not our thoughts and feelings frequencies also?

THE FREQUENCIES OF THOUGHTS AND FEELINGS

Since *everything* is made of energy, this means that your thoughts and feelings are frequencies too. So, naturally, scientists began to measure the frequencies of the brain. They found that in different states of thought and feeling, people produced what scientists call alpha, beta, theta or delta brain wave frequencies.

So, it's not money that has power. We give it power (energy) through our thoughts and feelings about money. After all, the dollar is just a piece of green paper. It's the combinations of thoughts and feelings that form the values of our society and make up our perspective about money. Money buys food, clothes, a roof over our heads and other essentials. It also buys many comforts in life. But, what price do we pay for money? Our global attitude towards money keeps millions enslaved to their desire to have more and more of it.

It has become one of the most coveted commodities of life. You could say that giving power to money is one "frequency perspective" of a collective global view about money. But within the global view are conflicting perspectives on who should get the money, how it should be used, who should be taxed, and how much. There is tremendous dissension in the world today over money. And that's just one cause of conflict. Our thoughts and feelings about our ethnic origin, our religion, national borders, and rights as people, form frequency perspectives that clash with the views of others. Conflicting frequency perspectives between people and nations are responsible for much of the discord in the world, including the raging ethnic wars in Yugoslavia today, the ongoing Catholic/Protestant war in Northern Ireland, and the powder keg of racial violence in the U.S.

More understanding of *frequencies* is filtering into the mass consciousness. You may have heard this common remark, "I just can't communicate with him. We're on different wavelengths (different frequencies)." Talking in terms of energy frequencies could sound like a foreign language, but it offers a new way of understanding and perceiving life. Once you understand that thoughts and feelings are really different frequencies of energy, then it makes sense to know which frequencies add to your power and fulfillment and which drain you. It is *your* power. You are the one who decides. Consciously — or unconsciously out of mechanical habits of thought — you determine where your power is going. How you direct your power is your responsibility.

We all have choice in our thoughts and feelings, and in how we use our energies. *We can choose our own frequencies.* As you understand this, you realize you aren't just a victim of this stressed-out world. Sure, the stress and circumstances around you are also energies that affect you, but you have a *choice* in how you react to them. And you have more power in your heart to manage your reactions than you probably know. You *can* achieve balance and fulfillment even amidst all the stress and fast-paced changes of today's world.

After the financial turmoil and Wall Street scandals of the '80s, many people realized that money doesn't buy peace, happiness and security, at least not in a complete way, not in a complete range or *band of frequencies.* Money can create a feeling of security in *one isolated frequency only.* It's a false sense of security because it's not complete. And when something creates a false sense of security, it also creates a sense of fear. With unemployment high and statistics showing more people living in poverty than at any time since President Lyndon Johnson declared "war on poverty," many people are asking, "What would happen if my money was gone?" For most people, that's a frightening thought. If your focused attention is on money as your security, then your security would be lost. That's the price we pay for making money our security. There are great fears about survival and tremendous stresses in the world today. It's no wonder. Money as a source of power has created a false security in millions of people.

When you understand how to be responsible for your thoughts and actions, you become empowered to make choices that lead to balance and fulfillment. Then you can build a *complete frequency band* of security within yourself. Self-empowerment is a step-by-step process that starts with self-understanding. It involves recognizing the inner power available to you and discovering how to direct your frequencies in ways that benefit you. It's like an inner mathematical equation: "When I have this attitude, that will be the result; $a + b = c$." It's streetsense math. Your thoughts and feelings form your attitudes and your know-how to cope with life. As you understand your mental and emotional patterns and habits, you will see where you lose energy, where you drain away your inner power and create fear, anxiety and insecurity within yourself. And you will also learn where your energy assets are, where you are building inner security and power that is not dependent on externals — on money, people, or events in life.

For the past fifteen years, I have researched, in-depth, the nature of the heart and self-empowerment with forty associates and friends at the Institute of Heart-Math™, founded by Doc Lew Childre. Everything we've learned, we've applied to our own lives. The results have been what people would call miraculous. We discovered which perspectives are empowering and lead to balance and fulfillment and which are depleting and lead to stress. We created wonderful, fulfilling and relatively stress-free lives, regardless of job circumstances, family backgrounds or the world situation. Having proved how it can be done in our own lives, we wanted to share our understanding with others. The HeartMath system is the result: A step-by-step method that any-one can apply to achieve balance and fulfillment. This system has had a dramatic, positive impact on the lives of many individuals, families and businesses. As you *practice* HeartMath, you unfold the hidden power of your heart in a regenerative manner. You plug your physical, emotional or mental energy leaks as you go. Then you don't run out of gas before you find your ful-fillment.

What type of power can change the stress-produc-ing attitudes and perspectives of this world? Common sense would tell us that a power *stronger* than our ha-bitual thoughts and feelings would be required. Our research at the Institute found that power to reside within the heart. It's a hidden power that operates in a higher range of frequency bands than the mind. In dif-ferent words, religions and native cultures have talked for ages about a higher power within. But why has this power been so hidden, so mystical? Why has it eluded us as a society? And why is the heart so often dismissed as merely sentimental or poetic? Perhaps the heart is just disguised with simplicity.

Is it really possible, you may wonder, that there is a hidden power of the heart so magnificent, so potent, so intelligent, so available, that it can help even *you* achieve balance and have fulfillment in life? At the Institute what we proved in our lives is that everyone has this power within. The heart is the *conduit* for this power of fulfillment. It *is* the place of contact for your source of power.

THE POWER SOURCE

Most people refer to their source of power as God. Some don't use the word God, calling it the Light, a Divine Force, Spirit, Higher Power, etc. All are referring to something past what ordinary human thoughts and feelings can understand. While many feel we live in a Godless society today, a society without much hope and in which spiritual and family values have declined, a majority of people *still* believe in God.

A 1985 national public opinion poll for US NEWS & WORLD REPORT showed that 90% of Americans believe in God. A more recent Gallup & Castelli poll put the figure at 94%. The poll also found that 90% pray, and 80% believe God still works miracles today. So, people believe there is an answer somewhere to today's woes. They believe, they hope, and they are looking for help.

To the majority of the world, God is associated with

Moses, Christ, Buddha, Krishna or Mohammed. All of these great teachers gave guidelines to help people find God. They taught different doctrines, but each spoke about the heart. Whatever your religion or *cherished belief*, the heart is the access point in the human system for experiencing God. It's also the place inside where you experience communion with Jesus, Buddha, Krishna and your fellow human beings.

All people have a heart, regardless of their mental abilities, nationality, race or religion. All people want love. If there is one thing that great teachers down the ages have asked of people, it is that we love each other. If we really did, would society be in the stress mess it's in today? Would there still be so many religious divisions and wars or so much racial, ethnic and personal strife?

We are always being reminded of the importance of love. Psychologists, educators, scientists, atheists, and people from all walks of life acknowledge the need for love. Our songs proclaim that love makes the world go round. There are 15,000 books in print in the United States alone on the subject of love. Yet, do people feel loved? Do *you*? I had to ask myself if I really felt loved. When I couldn't totally answer, "yes," I became determined to find out what love really is. This book is about my discoveries.

LOVE

The hidden power of the heart is love. Love is the core frequency or energy with which God created all. Most people intuitively know this. Whoever or whatever God is, most people agree that God is Love, and believe that

God was directly involved in the creation process. That Higher Power and intelligence gave each one of us a spark of God, of love within, to unfold, develop and become. How can we verify this? It is through managing our mental, emotional and physical energies from the heart that we can connect with this higher power and intelligence.

Each religion offers prescriptions for love and how to achieve balance and fulfillment — peace on Earth. The Bible says: "He that loveth not, knoweth not God; God is love," (1 John 4:7-8) and "If we love one another, God dwells in us and His love is perfected in us." (1 John 4:12.) The ancient Hindu bible, the Bhagavad Gita, says, "The Lord resides in the hearts of all beings," and "I am the God of Love."

When there's too much stress in your mind and emotions, it's hard to feel love, the hidden power in your heart. People marry for love, but statistics show half of the marriages end in divorce. Of these divorced families, 70% have children, and over 50% of these children feel responsible for the divorce, feel unloved and rejected by at least one parent. Children who don't feel loved have developmental problems and mental/emotional imbalances. Many teenagers who take drugs say they feel unloved, hopeless, and alone. Something seems to have gone wrong with love. Or, perhaps the real power of love has gotten buried beneath the stress of daily life and it's time to *really* find it.

Most people have never known how to self-activate the frequency of love within their hearts and keep it going. Many don't even realize this is possible. People look for love everywhere outside themselves, but where do we feel love? We feel it in our hearts. We don't say, "I love you with all my head." We say, "I love you with all my heart." We go to our hearts when we want to express our love. When love uplifts the mind or embraces us in sex, that feeling can be traced to a warmth, an energy in the heart. So what are the frequencies of the heart that radiate from love? We asked ourselves this question at the Institute and set out to discover what those frequencies actually are.

It's natural for people to discover some of this power of the heart in times of crisis — such as after the death of a child, rejection by a loved one, or when we bottom out in pain, anguish and despair. When there is no other place to turn, people do go to their own hearts and comfort themselves the best they can. Through prayer, meditation, a walk on the beach, we try to get in contact with our deeper self, an inner wisdom to give us some release. We listen for a still small voice inside, a voice of intuition or spirit. We try to tap into the highest source of intellect that we can find in ourselves to stimulate our understanding ability. This effort to go deep within the heart for an answer has been known to help people change their perspective and outlook on life. So what is this inner heart? And, how *can* we contact this magnificent force within? Read on.

Chapter 2

The Heart

When I first met the people who would later form the Institute of HeartMath, I was impressed by their sincerity, commitment and openness. Still, all the discussions we had about the heart and head, about God and the universe, seemed like scattered pieces in a giant jigsaw puzzle. How did it all fit together? Different religions and spiritual paths attempt to help people put the pieces together to a degree. We studied many of them along the way, and I kept looking for examples of people who had put their puzzle together, who enjoyed balance and fulfillment in their lives. They seemed few and far between.

At times, I questioned whether the heart my friends and I were talking about really did exist or was a product of the imagination. What was behind the expressions, "follow your heart," "get to the heart of the matter," "he plays with a lot of heart," or "go deep into your heart to find the answer"? Were they figures of speech or did they mean something more? Was there some reservoir of the heart that was common to all people, yet unexplored?

All I really knew about the heart was that it had the power to stir deep feelings inside that moved me to want to understand life, experience love deeply and care for others. One evening, back when I was still in college, a man I'd dated a few times asked me what God was. Out of my mouth popped, "God is love." That surprised me, but in my heart I knew it was true. There was an inner knowingness, a feeling of confirmation and peace that I felt *in my heart*.

IMAGINATION

As I learned more about the heart, I also discovered more about what was imaginary and what was real. I'd majored in pottery in college, with a minor in design, and I knew that imagination is the ability to form a mental image of something not yet present to the senses or something that has never been wholly perceived in physical reality. It was a thrill to me to capture a design as it would come to me in my mind's eye, and then give it physical shape and form. I'd taken classes in child development before settling into my major. They taught me that imagination is highly active in most children but tends to become inactive as we grow older and learn to confine our thoughts to linear thinking in school, work and social interaction. Yet, I knew the imagination was a valuable resource, a creative faculty that can take us way past fantasy into an exploration of the real. I was fascinated when I learned that Einstein said his Theory of Relativity, which led to the equation E=mc², came from visualizing beams of light, gravity and force fields. He would explore the whole universe in his imagination, then write down his ideas on the backs of old envelopes and paper napkins. His imaginings were so far ahead of the rest of the world that it was said only six people could understand his relativity theory when it was first published, and many rejected it. Nevertheless, it changed the course of history.

As I searched for more understanding of the heart and the imagination, I saw TV news reports about clairvoyants hired by the police to locate stolen property. They could see where the missing article was in their imagination and lead the police right to it. I read articles about people who had accurate precognitive visions and were able to save their own lives or their loved ones as a result. I studied documented accounts of near-death experiences in which people saw angels or visited other worlds. These people gave further confirmation of a reality beyond the senses that can be perceived with the imaginative faculty. As Einstein did from his armchair, these people who'd been near death brought back widened perspectives of reality — not of the type that would transform science, but perspectives that would change their own lives.

A 1982 Gallup poll found that *eight million* adults in the United States have had a near-death experience, and that was considered a conservative estimate. The vast majority of these people reported striking similarities in their experiences. They tell of traveling out of the body through a tunnel at a very fast speed; being bathed in a brilliant light that conveyed feelings of peace, joy and love; seeing beings of light and deceased loved ones; and watching their entire life flash before them in minute detail. After they come back from this experience, they want to help others. Many make major lifestyle changes. They become nurses or social workers or volunteer for community service. They have a fervent desire to see conditions in the world improve. Love, care and helping others is what matters to them now. They become less materialistic and no longer fear dying. I was intrigued by the transformation in these people and wondered, "What had moved them so deeply?"

The AMERICAN JOURNAL OF PSYCHIATRY recently published a paper on the near-death phenomenon. From this paper I could see that these statistics were arousing a serious scientific interest. Several controlled scientific studies are now in process. Only ten years ago, almost all scientists dismissed near-death experiences as hallucinations or imaginary, wishful thinking. But, as psychologist Kenneth Ring put it, "They can't all be making it up." Dr. Bruce Greyson, director of in-patient psychiatry at the University of Connecticut, summarizes current thinking, "The hard evidence we have all points to the fact that this is not fantasy."

THE MATH OF THE HEART

One day, I heard some of my friends refer to the heart as a computer. I questioned the theory and felt almost defensive. "A computer? How cold. People are not computers!" But I tried to be open and assess what they were saying without judgments. I listened to what they called the "math" (their data, information, and knowledge) to see if they really did have a wider perspective.

They explained that the heart contains an unlimited source of higher intelligence programs for making efficient choices in life. You can access these programs by listening for that still small voice (or intuitive feeling) inside you that gives you a sense of inner knowingness. You can then test the wisdom of what you perceived in real life to see if it brings more peace and understanding. The heart can bring in the highest intelligence — called *heart intelligence* or heart power — a power that illuminates understanding. The head, or mind, then translates the frequencies of this intelligence into intuitive thoughts, words or images so you can understand. The mind really acts as a subterminal to the mainframe computer in your heart. Your heart's intelligence has a wide, all-embracing perspective permeated with the frequency of love. A total understanding of all can come only from using your heart — your mainframe access to the universe.

A MAGNIFICENT JOURNEY INTO THE HEART

As I tried to understand this more deeply, questions would continually come up in my mind like, "What is the universe about?" "Why are we here?" These are questions we've all asked ourselves. So I said to myself, "Okay, heart, if there is an intelligence that somehow resembles the functions of a computer, I'd like to understand it." I closed my eyes and, using my imagination, I focused all my energies in that core place where I'd felt my heart stirring before. I visualized my heart as the mainframe of a computer and my head as the subterminal. I deeply felt I would see an inner image of how this worked, since I'd seen subtle energy forms and patterns several times before while sincerely praying, meditating or contemplating. But this didn't prepare me for what happened.

As I focused attentively on the core of my heart, I began to experience the heart as a pump for the life force, supplying me with vitality and contact with the energy of my spirit. I found my awareness moving into space and down a hallway with many doors. At the end of the hall, an image of seemingly infinite crystals appeared in a cornucopia shape. The cornucopia was filled with crystal-like formations. I saw many facets and edges. I realized that each crystal edge held a different intelligent frequency band. Each facet seemed to hold a different program or pattern. I was fascinated.

Then, the image became even clearer. Many colors swirled and changed, just like a kaleidoscope turning, gorgeous colors that created tremendous numbers of patterns that had depth, like a 3-D movie. I focused my attention on these patterns and saw them close up, just like looking through a magnifying glass. They formed round, intricate snowflake-like patterns that had shadow and light. I could see through them, and together they looked like a stack of floating computer disks but they didn't touch each other. I realized they were like a computer board where one disk electrically activated the next one. The crystal disks spun around, and the facets had grooves which electrically stored information just like computer chips. The crystal patterns seemed to go on for eternity, as far as I could see.

Suddenly, a profound insight came to me from some place deep in the core of my being. To my amazement, I realized that each individual human being has their own particular heart crystal pattern and colors and I saw this as the *soul's blueprint*. There were chips that contained detailed information: storage records of this life, past lives, and future possibilities — the whole intelligence of a human being. According to the choices that people make, the next program or next disk is activated. Each disk is like a chapter in a book, a chapter in a person's life. I now understood how people could see their entire lives replay before them at the point of death. I clearly saw that the total, compact intelligence of each human being is contained in a holographic formation of crystal-like computer chips in the heart. It was beautiful, elegant, and pristine. Love was the overwhelming feeling embracing my entire experience.

THE HEART COMPUTER

Later, I thought about how the heart computer functioned a lot like the computer at the office. I'd put in a disk, select a program, and somehow the mainframe would read the information that's electrically stored in the micro-chips inside. On my visual screen would appear the contents of the program that I'd selected. The computer would translate the electrical impulses, the frequencies, into color, images and words I could understand. I suddenly comprehended that the human mind is like a computer screen that gives a read-out of data that is input from our five senses, from our brain neurons and cells, and from our heart computer.

My personal computer at home happens to be connected into the publishing company's main computer network. In an intuitive flash, I realized that *there is a heart mainframe, a main computer into which every person's heart computer is networked.* I saw too that love is the power flowing through the global network. At last, I understood how everything in life could really be connected. Love is the electromagnetic core frequency that runs the entire mainframe holographic computer of life.

As people activate a program in their heart computer disk, for example, a mother loving her child, the disk starts to spin. As the disk spins, emotional energy gets magnetized to it. If attachment sets in, and we put conditions on love, the crystal-like disk becomes covered with a murky film and the pure love energy can no longer radiate clearly through it.

I was enthralled and continued to practice focusing on the heart. As time went by I saw more clearly how the heart computer brings in higher intelligence to the human system. The higher intelligence of the heart operates in an entirely different range of frequency bands from the mind. *The mind becomes illuminated and functions at its fullest potential when it serves as a subterminal for intelligence programs directed by the heart.* I practiced and practiced focusing my energies in my heart core to gain even more understanding. I was able to go deeper by radiating out love while I asked questions about the heart, including the physical heart.

Everyone knows the physical heart is the muscle that pumps blood through the physical body. The physical heart far surpasses all known motors in efficiency and design. You can be brain dead but the heart can still beat with life force. But if your heart stops beating, your brain dies quickly. The heart beats on its own. How? Even science can't answer that question yet. Engineers can hardly imagine how to improve on the blueprint design of the physical heart, even with their most ingenious and advanced machines.

In *Nutrition Plan for High Blood Pressure Problems* (Bircher-Benner), C. Hocrein describes with clear appreciation what this blood-pumping muscle really does for us on the physical level of life.

> "It works without interruption for 70-80 years, without care or cleaning, without repair or replacement, day and night. It beats 100,000 times a day, approximately 40 million times a year, and within 70 years supplies the pumping capacity for nearly 3 billion cardiac pulsations. It pumps 2 gallons of blood per minute, 100 gallons per hour, through a vascular system about 60,000 miles in length—$2^{1/2}$ times the circumference of the earth."*

This description tremendously widened my appreciation for my own physical heart. Like most people, I often just took it for granted. Now, I realized that the physical heart is a powerful machine made of muscle and tissue, designed by some incredible intelligence. That put to rest any lingering concern that the inner heart was coldly computer-like in its design and functions. It was becoming obvious to me that some higher intelligence was at work in the precise, mathematical organization of the universe — in the design and ordering of stars, physical bodies, atoms, gravity and all other particles and forces. I even read in a recent issue of GOOD HOUSEKEEPING how the tiny genes in the human body function as electrical switches. The combina-

---

* Bircher-Benner, *Nutrition Plan for High Blood Pressure,* (Jove Publications, 1977.)

tions of genes that are switched on or off decide the DNA programs for the development of all cells in the body — what organs they will become, what color eyes you will have and all the rest of your physical characteristics. The genes hold your blueprint and carry out their functions in an efficient, computer-like manner.

OPENING THE HEART

My admiration of the physical heart caused me to wonder more about the energy and intelligent properties of the inner heart. So one night I asked myself, "If all physical properties are made of frequencies, what kind of frequencies make up the non-physical inner heart?" I focused on my heart center and I noticed I felt more balance, peace, love and fulfillment. I realized these feelings were coming from the electrical energy system surrounding the physical heart. Talk about a natural high! I wanted more of this.

I asked my heart computer how I could sustain those good feelings in my day-to-day life. I soon found out how. The very next week at work, my boss offered me a new managerial position and told me to think about it for a few days. At first I was excited, but as I considered all the responsibilities of managing a retail food store I began to feel lots of insecurities about the job. My mind took every concern and mulled it over and over. "Would I do well enough? Would people accept me as manager? Would I still have enough time for my family?" As the thoughts raced through my head, I became even more insecure. I tried to forget the whole thing and distract myself with something else, but I was drained and noticed I was accumulating more tension and stress. I had a headache that wouldn't quit. Could all that insecurity have done this to me? Despair set in. "What should I do?" my thoughts kept asking. I was stuck in a room in my mind with four walls and no door. My mind kept rehashing the negatives versus the positives about the job, and wouldn't quit.

Finally, after swallowing two aspirin, I remembered my heart and its higher intelligence for making efficient choices in life. Perhaps, if I really made an effort to release my insecure feelings, I'd get a clear answer. I focused energy on my inner heart computer, hoping to gain some wisdom and clarity. Then I started sending love. I loved the boss who offered me the job, the store clerks, my husband, my son, and myself. I felt better and realized that people often go to the heart to find understanding and reassuring feelings of security when times are tough. It wasn't any big deal. I remembered how I'd gone to my heart for comfort when my grandfather died. In those situations, other people's words of comfort don't seem enough to bail you out. The strength to accept and adapt usually has to come from deep inside. Now, by focusing on my real heart feelings, my answers became clear, buoyant and strong. I felt a serene knowingness that I should take the job. I felt secure about it.

As my understandings of the heart grew, I realized that society's mushy, sentimental associations with the word "heart" are such a limitation. We don't usually think to call on the heart day-to-day for strength or direction in the hustle and bustle of life. Why would we, when most of us tend to think of the heart as the flimsy, emotional part of us that often gets us into trouble? In these stress-producing times, most of us misperceive the heart, and miss out on its hidden power of guidance and wisdom.

My contact with the inner heart computer showed me that the heart is not just mushy, soft and emotional — not just something to think about on Valentine's day or when we're falling in love. The heart has many frequency bands of exquisite feelings that add to the texture and quality of everyday life. We have words to describe these frequency textures, like care, love, forgiveness and compassion. In one riveting moment in the heart, it all became clear — these heart frequencies were keys for unlocking intuition and more intelligent understanding in my life. I understood why all the great teachers and founders of the world religions told their followers to love and care for each other. Love and care are access codes to the deeper heart wisdom, to your higher intelligence programs. Heart understanding is a major shift past ordinary thinking. It gives a wider understanding than is possible with just the analytical or deductive process of linear thinking. You draw more heart intelligence into your awareness as you relax the mind and listen to your inner heart feelings. This process can give you high-speed answers for your big and small choices in life. The heart is a fountain of wisdom and intuitive suggestions, yet so few people know how to use it.

Your heart intelligence offers programs vastly different from the isolated mind programs most people live by. Ambition, judgmentalness, greed, hatred and envy are mind frequencies that have their roots in fear and insecurity. The mind runs programs of fear and insecurity when it is cut off from the heart. Without a heart connection, the mind is left on its own to build deductive programs to run our lives. As a child, I had heard that love casts out fear. Now I understood why. We really are creating our own lives as we go, by the thoughts and feelings we allow to operate in our system.

As I continued to practice focusing on the heart, I discovered which feelings activated the heart computer. My heart guidance would encourage me to try attitudes of patience, kindness, appreciation, humor, and fun. Each time I followed through, and applied the inner wisdom, I noticed that stress would disappear and I'd feel on top of the world again!

It really is each human being's *choice* of which thoughts or feelings we allow to run in our system and for how long. Sure, it doesn't seem that way. But with practice, you can learn to adjust your thoughts and attitudes. That's what self-help programs attempt to facilitate, but they'd work much better if the heart were included. Social programming and habit have trained most of us to live in the mind, caught up in frequencies of insecurity, worry, resentment and frustration, trying to figure a way out. Fear and insecurity are meant to be warning signals, alerting us to our need to take action to protect ourselves from harm — heart action! But, if we stay too long in these frequencies, we harm *ourselves* and dilute our energy resources. Our minds keep repeating these energy-draining thought patterns, and our lives stay stuck on the same old stress merry-go-round.

By choosing to activate and sincerely feel heart frequencies, like love, care and compassion, you widen your receptivity to the higher intelligence that these heart frequencies draw to you. In *feeling* them, you create a deeper *perception* of yourself and others. This activates the energy equation: Feeling + Perception = Understanding. Your heart and mind then work together in a creative joint venture.

Most people intuitively know this, but haven't had the step-by-step technology or tools to learn to constantly live from the heart. The heart is what gives you self-empowerment, resulting in self-security and self-esteem. Your heart intelligence is your real teacher — because it ultimately has to confirm or reject what any other teacher says.

HEART DIRECTIVES

Ever since I can remember, I had a yearning for something that would make me feel complete. I was raised as a Presbyterian and my family went to church every Sunday. We weren't very religious, but something about Jesus Christ and the feeling of belonging, of family, and of love that I felt at church confirmed something inside me. As a teenager I went with friends to other churches, first Catholic, then Baptist and Pentecostal. I was "saved," and I enjoyed the fellowship. Still, I had a yearning for a deeper level of fulfillment and understanding.

At church, they spoke about the still small voice. I'd pray and listen but was never sure which voice was the right one. With HeartMath, I have realized that the still small voice is that intuitive knowingness in the heart that brings a sense of peace and love and feels right. I experienced it more as a feeling than as a voice, though at times words would come to me also. It is what you could call a *heart directive* because it will give you the most efficient attitude and answers for choices you have to make in life. You access heart directives by quieting your mind, going to your heart computer and focusing on it while sending out love. Sometimes it takes a little time before you get a read-out of intuitive intelligence. I came to see this as the true process of prayer.

After I accepted that managerial job I realized how truly powerful a resource the heart is. I was determined to use my heart computer daily. Instead of trying to solve problems with my head, I would stop and connect with my heart intuition the best I could and try to find a heart read-out from that still small voice inside me. It was just common sense. The more I followed through on what my heart's instructions told me, the more effective and fulfilling my life became. The best part is that the voice of the heart gets louder and clearer the more you practice.

Each of us has our own personal puzzle to solve as we try to find our balance on the seesaw of life. Our experiences are *life geometries* — different configurations of people, things, events, situations. Your life geometries form a blueprint for your growth and evolution. Their purpose is to bring you more understanding and realization about yourself and others. You gain insight into your blueprint as you self-empower by acting on your heart directives. They are your system's most efficient form of feedback.

As you listen to your heart directives and act on what they tell you, you start to re-program and harmonize your entire mental and emotional nature to bring balance and fulfillment. It's cause and effect. The kind of energy you put out is the kind that eventually comes back. Or in Biblical terms, you reap what you sow. You create your own stress or fulfillment according to the programs and attitudes you run through your thoughts and feelings each day.

ASSETS AND DEFICITS

By practicing what we call at the Institute "the Doc's Math," I learned to identify the energy assets and deficits in my system. Certain thoughts and attitudes drained my energy and cut off my heart connection, while others brought me back in contact with my heart. Feeling the heart frequencies of love, care, forgiveness and appreciation always brought me closer to my inner heart. If I got stuck in judgmental head thoughts, resentments and "poor-me" feelings, my heart computer seemed inaccessible. But through practice, I was able to turn my focused attention to either heart frequencies or head frequencies, or a combination of both. It was my choice. I learned that we all have a radio dial inside and we can choose which frequency we turn the dial to. I realized that's what self-empowerment is really about.

When I was at work, closing out the cash register, taking inventory or balancing the check book, I certainly wanted my head frequencies functioning in full gear. When I was with my family or friends, or by myself, it felt better to my system to live in the heart feelings of love, care and peace. I learned to turn my radio dial to the heart and put out a lot of love, compassion and appreciation. The rewards were a deep sense of fulfillment much of the time.

However, certain situations could still upset me and catch me off guard. I'd find myself back in the head, justifying my reactions and forgetting that I even had a heart. For example, I never spanked or really disciplined my son when he was very young. At almost three years old, he was so wild and created so many disturbances, that friends told me if I didn't begin to discipline him, he'd soon be impossible to deal with. He was controlling my life. My mind wanted to justify all the ways I was a good mother, and then I felt sorry for myself. I cried and cried about it. There I was, full of self-pity, drained and upset. But my friends were speaking truth and my heart knew it. So I picked myself up and decided to start disciplining him by asking my heart intuition how to do it. Once I get a clear understanding of a situation, there's part of me that becomes like a warrior, and I carry out what I know to be true. So I did. What a turning point this was in both our lives! His behavior started to improve immediately. He knew I meant business, but he also felt my love. I could see how I was saving a tremendous amount of energy for both of us. Within a month he had changed completely. Within six months, the change had stabilized — he had become a beautiful child.

Work was another matter. In my position as a manager responsible for several adults, I would set policies. When they weren't followed and other people were affected, I'd have to say something. I'd use my heart intelligence to communicate as effectively as I could. Things went well until one employee began to arrive at work late several days a week — always with some excuse. I spoke with her about it twice. When nothing changed, I didn't say any more because I wasn't the confronting type. I found myself avoiding her and not feeling very good about it. The other employees were getting resentful and expected me to do something.

One morning I woke up realizing I might have to fire her and it upset me terribly. I'd been doing so well living in the heart, my life was going so smoothly, and now this. I felt angry at her and at life. I slipped back into my old habit of feeling sorry for myself. When I got home from work that day, I was worn out. I didn't even feel like looking to my heart for an answer. Resentful thoughts kept churning over in my mind, and I knew if I didn't do something they would lead me into more pain and stress. My own intelligence was telling me I had to act now. Like a soldier, I sat on my bed and tried to quiet my racing mind and at least neutralize my feelings. I decided to send love to this young woman who kept coming in late. I focused on my heart and sincerely felt love for her. I was able to let go of the resentments by understanding she had problems juggling children and work. As I went deeper in my heart, I could hear my inner voice say, "Why not set up a different work schedule for her? See if she would start work an hour later and, even though it would mean less pay, she would still be able to keep the job." Other than being late, she was a good worker and I knew the rest of us could handle the store the first hour of the day just fine without her.

What a simple answer! It felt so good. If she didn't want to do it, then I'd have to let her go, but at least I felt secure I had a fair alternative. Now it was up to her. The next day I called her into my office and proposed the new plan, with the provision that she agree to always be on time. She was so relieved and grateful that she kept thanking me and said she'd work harder to make up for that hour. That's exactly what she did and she was never late. This experience made me even more determined to get back into my heart more quickly in the future. All that wasted energy from unnecessary worry and stress, a stocking full of deficits, just because I didn't go to my heart intelligence at the beginning!

IT'S UP TO YOU

The experience of seeing the results of heart intelligence in your life acts as a booster rocket to motivate you to keep using your heart for a read-out on big or small decisions. You begin to see different life geometries as opportunities — either for empowerment and accumulating energy or for self-victimization and accumulating stress. It's your decision.

The basis of heart empowerment as a complete system for fulfillment starts with *remembering* to quiet your mind, go to your heart, and follow your own heart directives to manage the regular day-to-day situations of life. You realize *you* are responsible for how you manage your system. It's your own inner business. You achieve balance by listening to your heart directives and self-correcting your inefficient thoughts, feelings and attitudes with heart power. It's just common sense to go for that feeling of knowingness inside. Most of us have a lot of old programming to clear out and re-program with wiser energy-saving attitudes. No one else is going to do it for you. No one else is going to give you fulfillment. Your security lies within you, just waiting for you to find it.

The dance of life does not have to be a slow waltz. It can be any type of dance you want, but sometimes a waltz is nice. As you dance through life you can find the perfect rhythm and balance for you. If you don't run too fast or walk too slow, you can find a fun fulfilling skip. As you learn what creates assets or deficits in your system, you gain more power to transform what doesn't feel good to you. In HeartMath seminars, we teach people how to create a *personal energy management balance sheet*. You use the balance sheet by observing yourself each day to see what drained your energy (your stress-producing attitudes and responses to situations) and what added to your energy and well-being (your energy-accumulating attitudes and responses). You pinpoint each deficit and ask your heart how to turn that deficit into an asset. Then you use heart directives to make the most energy-efficient attitude adjustments.

Just as I was starting to edit this chapter, the Los Angeles riots broke out. In the aftermath of the Rodney King verdict and the burning rubble of South Central Los Angeles, people everywhere were asking themselves, "What can we do?" Rich and poor, movie stars and homeless, blacks, whites, Koreans, Hispanics, all were pitching in together to sweep up the debris and provide food and clothing to the riot victims. Community feeling was strong. People asked each other, "Why does it always seem to take a crisis to bring us together?" On the TV evening news, a volunteer street sweeper was interviewed. He was asked, "Do you think there's some way that we can care for each other and cooperate to prevent this from happening again?" He answered, "We need to go back to the basic core values and have more heart, more understanding and compassion for each other." This TV interview inspired me to write a little faster.

Understand that the heart is not just some quick fix. There are no quick fixes. But from my experience and the experiences of all my friends at the Institute, heart intelligence does provide sound answers and solid, long-term solutions. Everything else has been tried. Why not try going back to basics and really learn to love and care for each other at deeper, more sincere levels?

Chapter 3

The Head

So how does the head relate to self-empowerment? Most of us want more brain power. People spend thousands of dollars on courses to sharpen their mental skills. Have you ever felt overwhelmed by all the seminars, books and information available everywhere? Through computer data bases, we now can access volumes of details on practically any subject. Even if you studied 24 hours a day, you couldn't learn it all.

The brain/mind/intellect is a fantastic and complicated piece of machinery. For the sake of simplicity, I'll refer to them collectively as *the head*, since they operate together within a certain frequency range of intelligence called head frequency bands. The principal function of the head is to sort, process and analyze information. The head also assesses, calculates, memorizes and compares. It is a very important and useful part of your system, and you would have a hard time surviving without it. You wouldn't be able to think, drive a car, speak, read, write, or get around in life without a good head on your shoulders.

But, again, as wonderful as the head can be, when it's not connected with your heart frequencies and isn't running efficient programs, it creates a lot of stress. A recent survey of American workers revealed that 62% frequently experience mental tension and anxiety; 45% say they often experience headaches due to stress. Some of the most common stress-producing head frequencies are self-judgments and judgments of others, fear, envy, resentment and worry. Can you see how these mental attitudes and reactions are by-products of comparison, assessment or analysis without the wider understanding of the heart?

Let me explain. Let's say you are envious or even resentful when a friend gets a lot of attention because of a new hairstyle. In that moment, you compare yourself and you don't feel very attractive. Or someone at work gets a compliment for a job well done and you don't, so you feel hurt and unappreciated. But, if you activated your heart, it would give you the security to realize that a compliment for another person doesn't take away from you. In your heart, you'd remember that a lot of people get fussed over when they change their hairstyle. Your heart would know that you've received compliments for your work at other times and that you can be glad for others when it's their turn to be acknowledged. These are simple examples of how the hidden power of the heart can help change your thoughts and save you from the subtle stress of self-judgment and insecurity.

While the head is a beautiful piece of machinery, far too much emphasis has been given to its development without the proper tools for its management. Our educational systems emphasize head knowledge instead of heart wisdom. It's the combination of both that brings higher intelligence, balance and the real understanding needed to reconstruct our society. The head and heart frequencies are designed to work together. When the unmanaged head operates without the wisdom of the heart, it often creates distorted perspectives, resulting in stressful thoughts and emotions. On its own, the head just doesn't have a wide enough range of intelligence to achieve a frequency perspective that creates balance and fulfillment instead of stress. That's what the heart is designed for. Without the heart involved, the head processors often won't shut off, like an old LP record stuck in a groove or a cassette tape in an endless loop.

MANAGING YOUR HEAD

In your conscious mind, thoughts run rampant a lot of the time. Have you ever come home after a long day at work, or after a misunderstanding with someone, and found yourself still thinking about what happened? Sometimes you know you're out in left field and you'd like to just stop it, but you can't. So, maybe you have a couple of drinks, or look for some other kind of stimulation to try to shut off your head. But even if this works for a while, the thoughts soon come back, sometimes in the middle of the night and even stronger than before. This is because the true addictions in life *are* our thought patterns. Physical addictions to alcohol, drugs, etc., often result from our urge to escape unfulfilling thought patterns. These addictive thoughts become realities we are creating, resulting in stress and wear and tear on the human body. They never bring peace of mind.

Take a look at this common scenario: First you feel frustrated with someone, then you assess their faults, then you feel justified in your feelings, then the anger starts and the negative thought patterns spin, obscuring your view of reality. That's a typical example of a head program running in a loop. Each time the loop goes around, your thoughts increase in speed, intensifying your emotions. So you convince yourself that things are even worse than you first thought.

In his popular book, *Healing The Shame That Binds You*, John Bradshaw explains, "Mental obsession, going over and over something, is part of the addictive cycle."* When emotional energy is added to your head processors, they spin and spin and, like a magnet, attract additional, similar thought patterns. Another example: If you are late for work and then an important business deal falls through, it's likely you won't have much patience in the traffic jam going home. When you arrive home, it's also likely you will carry those impatient, frustrated energies with you and they will affect your wife, your children, the rest of your night and possibly the rest of your life.

There are several ways to stop negative head processors. You can divert your attention to something else that your mind finds more stimulating (although the negative processors usually come back later). You can

---

* John Bradshaw, *Healing the Shame that Binds You*, (Health Comm., 1988)

stop when your system finally crashes — physically, emotionally, or mentally. Or you can consciously choose to stop negative thoughts by practicing specific tools that help you switch your frequencies.

The last alternative is obviously the most efficient. You can't necessarily change the *events* of the day, but you can *stop* your negative reactions to them. The first step is realizing that negative thought loops will only accumulate more stress. If you don't stop them, negative attitudes and patterns will continue to cycle through your system and color the rest of your day. You can practice transforming these energies by making an effort to go back to your heart power to at least *neutralize* your thoughts until you gain a wider perspective and deeper understanding. The ability to even neutralize negative mental and emotional patterns saves you a lot of stress and prepares you for the next step in heart empowerment.

"Well, maybe this will work with minor problems," you might say, "but some things are really major and very complex. How could the heart possibly provide a perspective that would really make things better? What if I were in a car wreck, or I lost my job?"

If an event is extremely disheartening, it can be a serious shock to your system. Accidents, job loss, divorce, illness, death, catastrophes, are all events in life that many people feel are impossible to accept or make peace with. But eventually, they usually do (often after many years). Finding heart understanding is always part of the process. Nobody really wants to stay in pain, but it can be very hard for the mind and emotions to let go of the head frequency perspective that keeps the pain alive. It takes an infusion of heart power to do that.

The heart understands that it can take some time to find peace in a crisis situation. Using your heart intelligence will speed up the process. The efficient way to dissolve the pain is to go back to the heart for a deeper understanding rather than let the head processors run wild and distort any insight your heart wants to give you. You achieve this by keeping the mind in neutral, so that the heart has a chance to give you a read-out. Putting the mind in neutral means simply trying not to think anything about the particular subject anymore. Just make an effort to put it on the shelf, still your mind and "be" the best you can until you can feel your heart again. *This isn't burying the problem.* It's having the hope and understanding that allows your heart to give you the love and intelligence that can help.

The longer you let negative thought patterns run, the more intensified they become and the harder they are to stop. You don't have to let stress build and accumulate to the point of anguish, tears of despair and numbness. That's where unmanaged head processors can and do take most people in a crisis. Once numbness sets in, release seems far away, and the process of *recovery* feels like it will take forever. It can take people months, years, sometimes their whole lifetime to forgive and make peace with an event. (Some people never do.) But, by managing your head processors with your heart, a release will come so you can survive and move on with your life.

There is hope! You do have choice. Whatever is happening to you — whether it's a problem with a person, a place, or with thoughts that arise from a past memory or a future fear — you have choice on how you process the experience. Your perspective in the moment will influence which direction you take. Your most efficient course of action is to go to your heart and gain the widest possible perspective. Don't just assume you know what to do from your first head reaction.

HOW WE MAKE MOUNTAINS OUT OF MOLEHILLS

Let's take a deeper look at how head processors work. If you've just received bad news — let's say your child got poor marks at school, or a business deal you were counting on fell through — it can be a disappointment that deeply affects your feelings and emotions. As your feelings signal a disturbance, your head formulates the news into thoughts and creates a frequency perspective. If you don't manage your head at this point, it will start its mechanical program of running mental tapes based on that perspective — usually tapes of dismay, frustration, self-pity and so on. The head magnetically calls up from memory similar experiences you've had, which reinforce that frequency perspective. Then the head program keeps running that perspective in a loop, adding energy to the loop, building the problem into a mountain, a crisis, instead of just a small bump in life. The unmanaged head can act just like a computer that runs out of control due to a program virus.

When you find yourself in a loop, it's time to go back to your heart — pronto — and get a new program from the mainframe. The heart program *will* bring in a more powerful frequency that feels better to your system. Then the head will dutifully formulate that frequency into *new thoughts* to give you a *new frequency perspective* of the situation based on heart intelligence.

When I first began to observe how this process works in my own system, I became aware that I often experienced energies that affected my feelings before thoughts and processors would start up. Sometimes I would just feel insecure, seemingly for no reason at all. It was impossible for me to always understand what frequencies were affecting my feeling world. You might notice this at times in yourself, too.

For example, if you are sitting by a pond surrounded by woods, the frequencies might feel tranquil, peaceful and serene, affecting your thoughts in a positive way. If you are in a traffic jam in New York, with horns blowing and car exhaust irritating your sinuses, the frequencies might make you feel tense and nervous, affecting your thoughts in a negative way. You can start to regain a sense of security in a stressful environment by first finding an inner silence within yourself. (It's really not that hard. Your heart's right there waiting for you to ask it for assistance — even in New York City.) Then, if you ask your heart questions, you'll receive answers that give you more understanding of your feelings. A sense of security comes with understanding. But it does require practice to build that connection between your head and your heart.

Observing this process was a major breakthrough for me. Since childhood, if someone even spoke to me in a sharp tone of voice, I'd feel hurt, take it personally, and often cry. I was sensitive to their energies and didn't know if I'd done something wrong. Once, when I was around five years old, a friend's mother was driving us home from our ballet class. She stopped in front of a house, turned to me and asked crossly if this was where I lived. I felt so hurt that I said yes and ran out of the car, even though it was pouring rain and I lived several blocks away. I arrived home soaking wet. It never occurred to me she might have been having a bad day.

When I decided to explore the heart, one of the first things I wanted to manage was my over-sensitivity which often dragged me around the block in a cycle that was difficult to break. My hurt feelings were so real to me, I felt justified in having them. This would distort my perspective of the whole situation. When my head took control and processed the insecurity, it seemed forever before I could feel my heart again. Each time this happened I'd wonder why I kept doing that to myself. It wasn't until I started to follow my intuitive directives that I stopped identifying with my insecure feelings and began to find balance. Finding that sense of knowingness inside gave me a powerful connection with my inner security, enabling me to feel other people's hearts and see truth more clearly. It was a big insight to realize that my *insecure reactions to other people were draining away my power*. I finally realized that if people gave me a strange look or spoke in a strong tone of voice, it wasn't necessarily my fault. Very often, they were just under stress. The feeling of power that came into my heart as I learned to manage my over-sensitivity was deeply fulfilling.

It's great to use your head frequencies to gather information and data. Then your heart can take that information and give you a truthful perspective. That is what your heart mainframe is designed to do — if you use it. The head and heart — in joint venture — bring you knowingness, understanding, and release. It's also fun!

When you first start to practice going to your heart, a satisfying understanding may come right away, seemingly like magic, accompanied by a new heart feeling. The speed and timing of your understanding depend on your ability to control your conscious mind with the heart, calm down and find your inner silence. If you try this on minor problems along the way, you build an inner muscle you can rely on when major problems or crisis situations occur. Remember, the mind wasn't designed to manage itself; that's what the heart is for.

MANAGING UNCONSCIOUS THOUGHTS

Everyone has old, unconscious programs from childhood and previous events in life that are stored in the cellular level of their system. Our physical, mental and emotional natures are so intertwined that our cells actually remember old hurts and pains. That's why some memories seem so difficult to release. By using your heart computer, you can erase them. If you find yourself in a fog and can't seem to tell the difference between your head thoughts and heart perceptions, rest the head a while and give the heart a chance to work. The head may still try to keep fogging your view with thought patterns. Just practice bringing your focus of attention back to the heart, feeling love for yourself in the heart center. Even if only a partial understanding comes, be patient, keep practicing and soon life will feel better. Patience is a powerful heart frequency that helps activate the understanding you are looking for.

A close friend, Debbie, has a "24 hour" rule. No matter how difficult the problem may be, she's found that if she puts it on the shelf and tries to stay in her heart, within 24 hours an insight or solution nearly always comes. By telling herself that 24 hours is the longest it will take to feel better again, she can be patient and let the heart do its work. The more responsible you are in directing your conscious mind with positive thoughts from the heart, the more your spirit can speed up the process of learning and growing, and you can move on into a more fulfilling life.

Without the heart perspective, the unmanaged head will keep re-creating the same old negative thoughts and feelings from the unconscious cellular programs in your memory. These negative programs generate inharmonious energy and stressful experiences that deplete your vitality. Left unchecked, the recycling of unconscious negative programs accelerates the aging process, leads to disease and can even cause death.

CRYSTALLIZATION AND MIND-SETS

Crystallization is a process that occurs when a thought pattern becomes imprinted in the mind and body. When you become crystallized (or hardened) in your ways, you have no desire to see and understand a wider perspective or improve attitudes within yourself. You quit caring whether or not things change or get better. You become limp to life. Crystallizations often form around attachments to "belief structures," your concepts about the way things are. They can form around attachments to anything.

If you're attached to certain creature comforts, and

believe you've always got to have them, you lose the flexibility that you had as a child when you were always ready for adventure. Some adults will no longer go to the beach because they don't like getting sand in their clothes. Others will turn down a hike in the woods because they fear they'll be tired the next morning. New people and new ideas are a bigger challenge when you're crystallized in your ways. Life just can't deliver all the gifts it wants to give you.

Thought patterns race through the mind like wild horses that are hard to stop once they get going. But, there are places on the trail where the mind can balk, just like a horse that stubbornly refuses to go through a stream. These places are called *mind-sets*. The mind decides that it "knows what it knows" and leaves no room for new perspectives. Some good examples of this are: Once people were sure the earth was flat, but now we know it's been round all the time. Once people used to say that if man were meant to fly he'd have wings, but now there are jumbo jets. You probably know someone who has a hairstyle or wears clothes today that he or she "wouldn't have been caught dead in" ten years ago. How many people do you know who now have diets, lifestyles, beliefs or political views that they once criticized others for having? As life variables change, your perspectives and thought patterns have to be able to change too. Don't become stagnant in "knowing what you know." You only hurt yourself when you're not expanding and growing. Many people can't stand the thought of aging, but it's the crystallized thought patterns and inflexible mind-sets that age people before their time. You *can* break through and challenge your crystallized patterns and mind-sets. That's what evolution and the expansion of love are really about.

Can a home builder proceed efficiently without interfacing with the architect? The head can run off on its own without understanding the heart's real plans. If the head receives its directions from the heart and they work together harmoniously, you will put your house in order. Your head will become that "right hand assistant" you've always wanted. Functioning as part of your *higher* self or intuition, the head will formulate the energy of higher intelligence into thoughts and new perspectives. The mind becomes illuminated, enlightened, and functions at its fullest potential when it operates creatively in its intended capacity — programmed and directed by the heart.

History is full of stories of people who were thrust into positions of leadership and power when all they really wanted was to help the leader get the job done. They never quite feel suited to the responsibility of the top job and keep wishing life would go back to the way it was when they were the right-hand assistant. In a similar way, the head is not really fulfilled trying to run the whole show and often creates more stress for itself so the heart will finally take over. In the TV series *Star Trek: The Next Generation*, Captain Jean-Luc Picard demonstrates heart wisdom. He uses Data, a fantastic computer mind, as his assistant and Counselor Troy, who has deep heart feelings, as his advisor. He makes the final decisions based on heart wisdom — a joint venture between the head and the heart.

In today's world, millions of people are realizing that listening only to their heads is stress-producing and

that there must be a better way. As more people explore the hidden power of the heart, humanity will become aware of its potential for fulfillment. After all, it's
what our head *and* our heart both really want.

Chapter 4

Stress
The Social Disease

"We already know that being emotionally distressed, being constantly anxious or constantly depressed isn't so healthy," says professor of clinical psychology, Jonathan Shedler of the Institute of Advanced Psychological Studies at Adelphi University. But suppressing distress may be even worse, according to Shedler's new research, reported in the SAN JOSE MERCURY NEWS.

"It is not known what percentage of people who consider themselves psychologically healthy have hidden distress. Such problems are hard to detect in oneself, but they may appear in indirect ways such as unexplained headaches or stomach aches, or friends might notice that a person appears anxious or unhappy."

Many people who don't think they have stress just don't recognize the symptoms, or deny what's going on inside until they take a deeper look. Let's take a "stress check." How often do you have any of these symptoms of stress?

- ❑ feeling you have no time   (feeling rushed?)
- ❑ moodiness–lots of ups and downs   (feeling tired?)
- ❑ bored–lack of care   (feeling depressed?)
- ❑ quick to get irritated or frustrated (feeling anxious?)
- ❑ short tempered   (feeling angry?)
- ❑ feeling unloved or unliked   (feeling unfulfilled?)
- ❑ headaches–too much to cope with   (feeling disheartened?)
- ❑ can't shut your mind off and relax (feeling tense?)

All these symptoms of stress are like alarm clocks going off, signaling a person's non-efficient energy expenditures. They are your system's natural way of giving feedback, of telling you something needs adjusting. Do they sound familiar?

Stress is an important life factor to consider. Shedler found that people who were hiding unresolved anxieties even from themselves showed an unusual jump in heartbeat and blood pressure when doing stressful tasks. This can lead to a higher risk of heart disease. New research links anger to a change in heart function. As reported by the NEW YORK TIMES,

> "In the study, [Dr. Gail] Ironson and her colleagues measured the heart's pumping efficiency in 18 patients with coronary artery disease while they recounted an episode that still made them angry. As the patients recalled the episodes, the pumping efficiency of their hearts decreased an average of five percentage points; seven of the patients had a decline of seven percentage points or greater. Cardiologists regard a decline of that magnitude as evidence of a myocardial ischemia, a drop in blood flow to the heart itself."

Let's look at a few more studies and statistics. Yale University researchers found that, "People who react to situations with strong emotions, particularly anger, are especially likely to die of cardiac arrest." The American Institute of Stress reported, "Studies tie overproduction of stress-related hormones to unbalanced immune systems and to many health problems." THE JOURNAL OF NEUROSCIENCE published the results of a study that showed direct evidence that prolonged exposure to stress can accelerate the aging of brain cells in the same region of the brain affected by Alzheimer's disease, leading to impairment of learning and memory. Research conducted over a twenty year period by London University's Institute of Psychiatry found that people who bottled up their emotions under stress were likely to be more prone to cancer. Cigarette smoking or eating foods high in cholesterol by themselves had less effect in causing disease than did negative reactions to stress.

Stress is quickly proving to be the leading cause of death. Under stress, the energy in a person's system becomes short-circuited and their energy accumulators become drained. As stressful reactions to situations keep recurring, your entire system runs down. Everyone has their own threshold of *stress tolerance,* and that tolerance point is being reached by millions. Look around you. Look at our society. People are getting to the point where they no longer care much about anything and are just trying to survive. They are engaged in a constant effort to meet basic physical needs like food and water, warmth and shelter, a car and money for gas. Their main purpose in life is staying alive. When this happens, the mind becomes numb and dormant and can cross the line of sanity to protect the heart from sadness, despair and total heartbreak.

Stress is the mental and physical strain caused by having more to cope with than one can comfortably handle. The missing formula for stress relief is within your heart. Learning a procedure to de-stress as you go is a lot smarter than having to undergo some other procedure like open heart surgery, chemotherapy or radiation. It's your choice. You can prevent the latter if you learn to de-stress as you go. It's strong, unmanaged head frequency bands that block one's heart intelligence from being able to prevent and release stress. I know, because like most people I have some strong head bands. I feel things deeply, and if something hurts, my head willingly jumps right in to find out why. It can process and process, accumulating loads of stress if I let it.

WATCHING YOUR REACTIONS

Let me give you an example of what one of my typical stressful days used to be like. See if it resembles some of your own. I'd be awakened in the morning by the phone ringing, then a voice on the answering machine reminding me about the PTA meeting that night. I'd yell at the machine, look at the clock and see that I was going to be late for work unless I hurried. I'd rush to the bathroom, spill shampoo all over the rug, and get angry at myself for being so clumsy. I'd tell my son three different times to get out of bed, quickly throw together his breakfast, get exasperated because he couldn't find his homework again, help him find it, and send him off to school. Then, I'd grab coffee and toast for myself and run out the door, only to discover I hadn't put gas in the car. Frustrated and telling myself, "I can't believe how stupid I am," I'd wait in the line at the self-serve gas station, listen to the news report about the highest unemployment figures in years and try to fix my hastily applied make-up as I stared at the bags under my eyes in the rear view mirror. I'd get gasoline all over my hands as I filled the tank and have to smell it in the car all the way to work. By the time I'd get to work, several other ladies would be lined up outside the only rest room and I'd sit at my desk, heart pounding, blood pressure rising, already stressed-out, with the work day only just starting. Does this sound like any of your days?

At the Institute of HeartMath, we've come to see stress as an inharmonious energy or experience that *results* from our inefficient reactions. I had quite a few inharmonious experiences on the day I just described. By the time I left work, I was exhausted and felt like I had a tight band around my head. Remembering days like that, I understood what this definition of stress really meant. *It was my negative reaction to each event that determined the level of my stress.* My frustrated reactions to the minor everyday hassles created my stress and constricted the flow of my energy. I was the one responsible for draining the spirit out of me.

A constant dose of minor irritations and griping will feed back in your system over time, robbing you of your energy and vitality. It's really not the major crises that create the most stress. As I've said, in a major crisis, people do tend to go to their hearts. People seek out friendship and receive understanding from others. Just think of all the heart-warming stories of communities banding together after a disaster like an earthquake, flood, or fire. It's really the constant daily hassles that cause so many to say they experience high levels of stress. A recent Harris poll showed that 89% of all adults — 158 million Americans from all walks of life — experience what they call high levels of stress. Shelton Marketing Communications reported that 90% of all adults they surveyed said they experience high levels of stress once or twice a week; 25% experience high levels of stress every day. No wonder 75% of all doctors' visits are for stress-related complaints!

As a society, we tend to assume that continual irritations are a necessary part of life. Many business executives and managers still believe that high stress levels on the job are essential for productivity and a strong work ethic. But statistics are proving otherwise. Research is showing that our reactions to the "little hassles" release more negative hormones into the body and cause more disease than a single, big stressful event. Little hassles create "silent stress," constant negative inner mental and emotional dialogue (like judging yourself or others). This depletes your energy, accelerates the aging process and stifles inner growth and effectiveness. A build-up of reactions to little hassles can actually cause a more traumatic response to a major event later on.

Managing your reactions to stressful situations is the key to health and well-being. Stress is not just an effect. Stress accumulated in the system not only causes many major life crises — like divorce, a teenager in trouble, a heart attack, drug or alcohol addiction, and many other chronic human, social problems — but diminishes our ability to deal with them effectively. Pain is the result.

Pain is *louder* stress, a screaming alarm bell warning us that something's not right. Irritation + frustration + anger + judgment + resentment = a guaranteed formula for stress. A lot of stress eventually brings pain. When you overload your head computer with negative thoughts and feelings, you eventually "CRASH,"at which point you cease to function normally, mentally, emotionally, or physically. A crash can be excruciating.

After a crash people usually finally stop to ask, "Why?" "Why me?" or "Why does this *keep* happening to me?" Each person's system, because of their blueprint and their responses to events in life, will have various thresholds of stress tolerance. At some point, after too many inefficient responses, you can become so overloaded physically that your health deteriorates, or so overloaded emotionally that you choose suicide — death is your means to finally end the pain.

Life *is* a gift, even though it doesn't always appear that way. Sometimes life feels like a gift you want to return. It's often hard for people to understand why things happen — why they lost their job, or why they lost a friendship or a prized possession. How could a loss be a gift? Life is not necessarily what you would call a logical sequence of events. But even the seemingly illogical events actually have plenty of make-sense to them if you could see and understand the entire picture of your blueprint. As understanding comes and you fill in more pieces of the puzzle, life becomes an adventure — a dream come true. By using heart intelligence, you *can* discover your purpose in life.

THE STRESS EPIDEMIC

Stressors are stimuli that can cause physiological or behavioral changes in people. When people can't handle stressors efficiently, whether on the job or at home, internal *stress* results. Often we can't change our environment, at least not in the moment. We can, however, change ourselves so that we can handle our environment without creating stress in ourselves.

Ironically, many people who want to change the world become so frustrated, angry and resentful, they dilute their power to change the conditions that cause their frustration. You can see this in certain people in the environmental, abortion rights, equal opportunity and peace movements. This is not to say that we shouldn't work for social change. But by learning to manage our stress, we can increase our power to implement the positive changes we want to see.

Many people have told me they prefer to have some stress in their lives. It provides stimulation and motivation. They call it positive stress. At the Institute, we call this "creative resistance energy." It's different from stress. When you creatively respond to stressors or resistances, you don't experience stress in yourself. Instead, the stressor becomes a fun challenge, an opportunity for growth like weightlifting. You build a positive strength as you creatively respond rather than react. Then the stressor doesn't drain you. You feel good inside. Stress, on the other hand, never feels good, nor does it make for a fulfilling lifestyle. Stress ages you. It's the culprit, the ignition key to hundreds of diseases.

The power to think yourself into misery is within you, but the power to stop it is within you also. Lack of self-management is what can cause a massive stress buildup within a person's system. The mind bounces back and forth with thoughts — about the day, about the future, about the past, about "Where should I be?" "What should I do next?" "Which direction should I go?" and on and on. When the head gets going, it can seize on a thought and make a headstrong decision that is not easily restrained. If that decision doesn't work out as you hoped, you can feel miserable, defeated.

Global stress is accumulating at a faster rate in the '90s because of constant unmanaged head processors, nervous systems on overload, and the pressure to make fast decisions in a time of rapid change. As C. W. Metcalf, author of the book *Lighten Up*, says, "The ascending rate of change in society has made things tough every day. We're having to adapt more often, with less preparation, on more issues, than at any other time in history."* The struggle to make decision after decision has become so confusing and overwhelming that people are frustrated with life.

Turn on the evening news for an hour. You can count on getting a stress report on the economy, the environment, politics, and more. Over the last twenty years, mental labor has replaced physical labor throughout much of the world. As a result, mental stress has become epidemic. Businesses are reeling from the latest stress statistics. A survey by Northwestern National Life Insurance released in 1992 reported that: 34% of U.S. workers said they considered quitting their jobs because of excess stress; 46% described their jobs as

---

* C.W. Metcalf, *Lighten Up: Let C.W. Metcalf Show you How to be More Productive, Resilient & Stress-free by Taking Laughter Seriously*, (Addison-Wesley, 1992)

highly stressful (twice as many as in 1985); and 33% said they believe job stress will lead them to "burn out" soon.

Worker's compensation claims are climbing dramatically as a result of job stress claims. A typical stress case is likely to be twice as costly as the average industrial injury claim — more than $15,000 each in medical treatment and lost work time. In his book *Self Empowerment: The Heart Approach to Stress Management; Common Sense Strategies*, stress researcher Doc Lew Childre, founder and president of the Institute of HeartMath says,

> "It would startle most businesses to have a computer readout weekly, showing the amount of work-time their employees spent thinking and emoting over their problems. Then, if you had another computer readout showing the amount of negative hormones released into the body as a result of those thinking habits, and the health consequences, in the name of smart business you would want to make some mental and emotional adjustments. Computers can't generate all that data yet, so we don't have to face the facts. Yet, the facts of stress will find us — anyhow. The stress deficit accrues, whether or not we are conscious of it."

When we first introduced our HeartMath trainings for businesses, industry consultants confirmed that mental/emotional self-management *is* the missing link in their seminars, trainings and wellness programs. According to INDUSTRY WEEK magazine, for the sake of survival, as well as for bottom-line profit, "Employers ought to be begging to help people find the most enjoyable, fulfilling and creative way to do their job."

When you are exhausted, overwhelmed and stressed, your days aren't fun, adventurous or fulfilling at all. As stress sets in and isn't released, it wears and tears on your entire system. It wears and tears on the family, schools, businesses, government — the entire social system. There is great injury happening to individuals in our society today as a result of stress. Much of it occurs silently inside. It occurs inside the mind before it inflicts itself on others or on one's own body. There is a way out. You can start by learning to balance yourself, day-to-day, by using your heart computer — your higher intelligence. As you practice, you will discover that there is a place beyond suffering. You begin to see clearly that you can choose how you react to any situation in life.

Nine years ago, my higher intelligence began to instill in me a sense of purpose. I was exploring the pristine energies of the universe (the heavenly worlds) and deeply wished that I could convey the feeling of love I felt there to this world. There is no density, no stress or strain; there is a freedom that you can hardly imagine. There is a peace — that became my mission. "Peace on Earth, Goodwill towards Men." Through the hidden power of the heart, it really is possible to bring the peace of heaven to earth. As you learn to manage your day-to-day stress, you will find your next level of peace. Peace is the opposite of stress. Those two frequencies — peace and stress — cannot live in the same place as they cancel each other out. It is each individual's choice. The game of life is a game with you and you. You can *heart empower* yourself, once you know how. You can de-stress your life. It starts with de-stressing the simple, ordinary day-to-day hassles.

Spend a little time quieting your mind and asking

yourself, "During the course of a day, week, or month, do I accumulate more stress or more peace?" To recap: Start to recognize your mental and emotional response patterns. Observe and identify whether your response to stressors is from the heart or from head reactions. See where head reactions take you. Evaluate whether they are efficient or non-efficient expenditures of your energy, and then self-correct. Access your heart intelligence and apply what your own heart tells you to do — in your attitudes, your understandings, your communications with others, and your actions. With self-management you can achieve real peace and inner security in a stressful world.

Chapter 5

Higher and Lower Heart Frequencies

O ne of the biggest pieces of the puzzle fell in place for me with Christian, my 10 year-old boy. I love him dearly, but at times my feelings of love took me into insecurity and over-attachment. Like all parents, I wanted him to excel in school and be well-liked. When I'd hear reports of him acting in a mean way to someone, my heart would hurt. I'd take it personally and wonder what I was doing wrong. How can the heart hurt? Why does love hurt? Understanding, as I did, about the heart computer, this feeling of hurt didn't compute!

Millions of people today are afraid to love because they fear being hurt, rejected, and feeling the pain of a broken heart. Once burned, they don't want to touch hot coals again. Others see the heart as gushy, sentimental and getting them into trouble when they feel deeply about things. A lot of people have experienced so much hurt and disappointment, they have shut down their hearts in self-protection and feel detached, even numb. They have vivid memories, as a child or young adult, of opening their heart, only to have someone they loved trample on it. There are thousands of marriage counselors and therapists trying to help people re-gain a sense of intimacy in relationships. While our society values an honest, sincere heart, it is wary of the vulnerable, open heart.

I puzzled over this apparent contradiction. I wasn't going to stop loving and caring. What else is there? That would be denying what makes life worth living. I sincerely wondered how it was that my love and care could give me peace and happiness, then lead me into hurt and stress. Wasn't this the very issue philosophers, artists and poets had tussled with throughout the centuries?

My friends and I began to take these questions to heart — to the heart computer. As I focused on my heart and sent peaceful feelings of love to Christian, I realized I was leaking my power because of my attachment to what others might think. The *fear* that they might judge me or him was creating my hurt. It wasn't "love" that was hurting at all. By bringing those thoughts and fears back to my heart and just loving, I saw that people were only trying to help me. This gave me a huge sense of release. I also saw my child in a balanced way. Yes, there were areas where I could help him improve his behavior, but he really was a good kid who rarely caused problems. I realized it wasn't my love that had created my insecurities; it was my over-sensitivity which caused me to take things personally.

This answer was the tip of the iceberg for yet another understanding of the nature of the heart. At the Institute we discovered that the heart has both lower and higher frequency bands with all sorts of ratios and colorations in between. To visualize higher and lower heart frequencies, realize that the universe is filled with an infinite number of radio-type frequency bands. Each person is their own unique radio station, with their own pattern, design, colors, textures and sonics. Each individual's radio station is tuned to different frequencies at different times. While some frequencies affect us unconsciously and we can't do much about them, we always have choice in how we respond to the frequencies we are aware of.

Heart frequencies are the "feelings" you experience, and feelings are what make life worthwhile. Higher heart frequency bands are the higher aspects of human nature, feelings such as love, care, compassion, tolerance, patience, appreciation, and kindness. These frequencies are accessed from the core of the heart. The primary core heart frequency is "just love" or "just love the people," which we will talk a lot about. The higher heart bands are of a sincere and caring nature. They are always beneficial to your system and to others. As you broadcast these frequencies, they regenerate you throughout your day. They enhance your immune system and are the true fountain of youth.

Higher heart feelings don't compare; neither do they blame or judge. When you are tuned to these heart feelings, you realize that each individual is doing the best they can. Higher heart frequencies are the doorway to higher intelligence and wider comprehension.

HOW LOWER HEART FREQUENCIES AFFECT YOU

Lower heart frequencies are heart feelings colored with sentiment, attachment, expectations and overcare. Lower heart bands bring unpleasant feelings of worry, anxiety, hurt, and feeling sorry for yourself or someone else. When love turns into attachment, or compassion gets colored with sympathy, your heart energies are pulled into density, often feeding back in your system as hurt and sadness. Love can seem like the cause of that hurt, especially when the initial heart feeling is deep and sincere. In reality, it's what our head does with our feeling of love that determines whether it stays in the higher heart and is fulfilling or leads us into lower heart feelings and stress.

Care is a higher heart band that can easily slip into the lower heart band called *overcare*. I caught myself slipping into overcare while caring for a very sick friend. I could feel her pain, her worry that she was going to die. In the past, I would have worried and cried with her in sympathy. However, I knew that worry would only drain both of us. Instead, I activated the most sincere care I could feel from my heart and kept sending that quality of care to her. I was able to know when she needed liquid, warmth or a kind word. She became very peaceful and my own energies stayed in balance. At the end of the day, I was serene and she was sincerely grateful.

When you allow lower heart bands to take over your feelings, they can deplete your system and cause tremendous stress. People operate from the heart some of the time, but often believe they consistently do, when it's really overcare, attachment, sentiment and expectation they are feeling. These frequencies cut off your connection to your higher heart. They can easily lead to thoughts of worry, disappointment and fear. These thoughts then activate more feelings of insecurity, hurt and pain. That's why the heart is often perceived as being so vulnerable.

THE "BROKEN HEART"

When you have a "broken heart," your mind takes a deep disappointment and keeps replaying that same old sad movie, reinforcing the hurt feelings each time. A broken heart is really the result of a head-on collision between broken attachments, expectations, and emotional investment; there is some heart energy mixed in which is why it feels like your heart aches. You really did love, but then your love drifted into the lower heart frequencies of attachment and expectation — expecting someone to love you in the way you loved them. When that doesn't happen, the emotional shock can short-circuit your mind and your emotions. Your security was invested in someone outside yourself and when that security is gone, you feel like a victim, powerless.

While some people are able to connect with their heart power, resolve their pain and move on, many get stuck in this kind of crisis and never recover. The head replays the old hurt endlessly, or buries it in the unconscious so they can survive. When a child or adult is a victim of traumatic abuse, it's easy to justify holding onto hurt and resentment that come from a feeling of betrayal. But as natural as that may seem, holding onto hurt only causes self-victimization and more pain. When people finally let go of anger, grief or feelings of betrayal in their lives, it is the heart that has resolved the problem and released it from the mind. When bitterness, denial, and sadness are released, it's the higher heart frequencies that help you let go, usually bit by bit. Learning how to forgive, release and let go, is an important investment in mental, emotional and physical well-being.

The head alone cannot manage the emotions or heal the mind when it short circuits. The head can repress emotions, but those basic mental/emotional issues will pop up again and you can feel defeated. Only the heart has the power to give you complete release from mental and emotional issues that drain you. The bailout is to activate enough heart power to replace self-victimizing head programs with true heart programs. You start by activating your heart power to manage your attitudes and release inefficient head thoughts about your smaller problems in life. That builds your heart strength and power to then resolve your major problems.

EMOTIONS

"E-motion" is energy in motion. It amplifies or adds a charge to your thoughts and feelings. Emotion can be called the affective aspect of your consciousness. It is a gorgeous quality to have, a juice running through your system that provides that extra "feel good" to life — in color, sound, taste, smell and texture. But emotional energy in itself is neutral. It picks up its coloration either from the head or from the heart. Emotional energy can be added either to a disturbance or to a fun excitement. The heart says, "Let's Love," and the emotions say, "Yeah!" The head says, "Let's get frustrated," and the emotions say, "Yeah!" How we manage our emotions determines whether they add quality to our lives or bring us stress.

Too much emotion becomes emotionalism, the indulgence in unbalanced emotion. Emotionalism may feel good in the moment, but doesn't solve the basic problem. It can also drain the vitality out of your system. If you're at the point of tears because something has disturbed you, that's when you can choose to discipline your emotional body. You can let a few tears run down your cheeks — something evidently hurt. After that, if you get stuck in the head and blow it way out of proportion, you will drain your energy. Instead, you can go back to the heart and make peace with the situation. Then your heart will help you find a wider perception. Watch out — if your head keeps replaying the hurt, the disturbance will build into emotionalism. If you do that, you are indulging in a "poor-me" attitude and making the disturbance larger than it has to be.

Emotionalism will not solve a problem. To feel sorry for yourself, or blame the pain on someone or something else, will not dissolve the issue. It will only create stress. Do have patience and compassion for yourself. Don't be a poor me-er who is looking for pity and sympathy from others. You probably won't get the sympathy from where you want and expect it. And if you do, it will just be them crying with you. This won't free you from that emotional energy pattern. If you're truly in despair and sincerely ask for help, you will magnetize compassion and understanding to you. But, if you are in a childish pout and inner temper tantrum, you'll just build more stress until you collapse and release all the emotional energy you've accumulated. It's like having to close out your bank account because you couldn't stop spending. You have to start all over again from square one.

Emotionalism can also be created on the opposite side of the spectrum by over-excitement. While genuinely looking forward to a vacation or a special date, you can overload your emotional nature with anxiety, expectations and an impatient feeling of "can't wait." That overload unbalances your energies, blocking your heart flow. Quite often children build Christmas into a stressful situation by becoming over-expectant and over-anxious. Then they become tired and cranky because they've expended too much energy in over-excitement.

Don't build an expectation so huge that if what you're wanting doesn't happen you will be crushed or deeply disappointed. The answer is to discipline your system to be excited about an upcoming situation, a fun "can't wait," but in a balanced way. By using your heart to balance your emotionalism, you aren't shoveling the emotions under the carpet and pretending they don't exist. You're taking control of them so they work for you to keep the fun and adventure in life going your way.

People often use drugs, alcohol, food, sex, TV, or whatever they can find to try to calm their emotionalism. These diversions are only temporary and don't resolve the basic imbalances and lack of emotional management. Your emotions work best for you when receiving directions from the heart. By learning to watch for your lower heart pulls, you can start to balance your emotions. Notice how higher heart frequencies feel compared to lower heart and head frequencies. The feelings of true love and care are very different from feelings like attachment and overcare. As you practice bringing your emotional pulls back to your higher heart, you will gain a peaceful feeling of true love, care, or compassion.

Many marriages are based on intimacy, but when this turns into physical or emotional attachment couples often become insecure and the relationship can get sticky. The stickiness often causes one partner to want to pull away. By learning the difference between this isolated frequency of intimacy, and all the other frequencies of the real heart that are clear, compassionate and caring, you can bring new love, depth, and fulfillment to a marriage.

As you understand your higher and lower heart frequencies, you start building an efficient relationship between them. Your experience of life deepens as you bring your energies back to the higher heart as soon as you notice unsatisfying feelings. Your intuition will wisely guide you into the balanced and intelligent heart frequencies of true love.

SOCIAL CHANGE

Let's consider these levels of the heart in relation to society. Society is full of examples of lower heart frequencies and the stress they bring. Because of stress, many people are now waking up to the fact that our culture has placed an overemphasis on developing the head and mind. As a result, our social structures have reached a ceiling in awareness which they cannot go past without understanding the heart. Throughout the ages, religion has helped people develop the heart to some degree. But by the time of the Industrial Revolution, human mental development had reached a point where much of the traditional religious dogma no longer made a lot of sense to the rational mind. As the head charted its own course, the heart was left behind. Now, escalating stress is forcing people to look more deeply within to find their own common sense and inner security. Back to the basics, the heart. As people wake up to the fact that the mind works more effectively when directed by the heart, the next level of social change can happen rapidly.

You don't have to wait for society to rediscover the heart before you achieve balance and fulfillment. You can start now by practicing heart management in ordinary day-to-day situations. Consistently activate your heart power. This is done by loving people more. Do it when you're on the phone, running errands, at home with the family, or anywhere. Send a feeling of love to whomever you encounter. Go to your heart computer to make sense of the daily events that are puzzling or stressful. Let your head give you creative readouts of your intuitive heart directives. Your heart and head will soon function as a highly intelligent team, with the heart in command. As Joseph Chilton Pearce, noted author of *Magical Child,* states, "The affairs of the heart are directly connected to the brain and it's the heart's natural intelligence that must be unfolded for the brain to operate with greater efficiency."* The hidden power of the heart is simple. You just have to start to use it.

* Joseph Chilton Pearce, *Magical Child,* (Bantam, 1981)

In Chapter 8, we'll explore some power tools that will enable you to maintain deeper contact with your own heart power. The power tools will activate your higher heart frequencies to increasingly widen your perspective of life. They are business tools — the business of managing and re-creating your own system. Higher heart frequencies bring the essence of real wisdom. They are part of your (and the world's) heart computer software and DNA blueprint for evolution. Using the tools is essential in the unfoldment of these heart bands, but you must remember to use them. "Just Love the People" is the core heart frequency, your mainline power tool, encoded with light, power and intelligence. In Biblical times it was expressed as, "Love ye one another," and "Love is the fulfilling of the law." Both sayings refer to the power of the primary core heart frequency. As you increase your heart awareness, you will gain the compassion and understanding to help others dissipate stress. With sincere practice, you *can* achieve peace and fulfillment.

Perhaps it's through continually activating these higher frequencies that we can gain more intelligent understanding of God — the ultimate power source. My perception would be that God sees this world as one big yard. We are one big family of people, trying to make our way through the unfolding puzzle of life. We are all connected to one another in the heart. Connecting with the ultimate source of love is possible through discovering the hidden power in your heart.

Chapter 6

The Dimensional Shift

M any business leaders and trend forecasters are saying that the world is going through a *paradigm shift*. Some are calling it a *dimensional shift*. A paradigm is a model of how we view reality. A paradigm shift occurs when our fundamental view of reality changes to a new, wider perspective. An example is when masses of people realized that the Earth rotates around the Sun and is not the center of the universe. That changed the entire global perspective, opening up new potentials never before dreamed of. When Einstein proved all matter is energy, another paradigm shift occurred, heralding breakthroughs in science and technology that otherwise would have been impossible.

A current paradigm shift is the movement in business away from the perspective of just money and profit to an emphasis on excellence and quality. As Joel Barker, author of *Future Edge*, observed in an interview in

INDUSTRY WEEK magazine:

> "Total quality is a paradigm shift. There's going to be a dramatic separation between those who practice Total Quality and those who pretend it. The winners will be the world-class providers of products and services.... The Total Quality people will see results that are exponential.... The base of the twenty-first century is built on excellence."

A *dimensional shift* is made of many paradigm shifts unfolding over time. Although science speaks of dimensions just in terms of time and space, a dimension is actually a specific frequency range of perception and intelligence. Each dimension embraces the intelligence of the dimensions below it and can be perceived as its own world of energy and form.

THE THIRD DIMENSION

Our physical reality, including our dense physical body, exists in the *third dimension*. Newtonian physics led people to believe that the only "reality" is what we can perceive with our physical senses. Our senses perceive every piece of matter as separate, leading us to conclude that everything is separate. Adopting this paradigm view, many scientists closed their minds to the possibility of another reality. This is an example of *third dimensional* perception and intelligence.

One way to better understand dimensions is to realize how human awareness develops. Newborn babies come into the world with limited conscious awareness. They are totally dependent on their mothers for food, shelter, moving around, etc. As the child develops, her awareness expands on physical, mental and emotional

71

levels. Soon she can walk, talk, feed herself, think, and speak. Before long she can understand more complex ideas. But for most people, the development of awareness slows down. It hits a ceiling in the third dimension; only through greater understanding can we break through this ceiling.

Ordinary day-to-day human awareness is a product of the third dimension. We tend to perceive things as good and bad, right or wrong, black and white, and react accordingly. Often we view conflicts as, "that's the way things are and it's going to get worse." The third dimension is a range of frequency bands that's bound by many illusions of limits. These boundaries are colored by fears that keep us from seeing a way out. They're created by thoughts like, "There is no proof of life after death, therefore there isn't any life after death." You probably know people who are afraid to even think about life after death.

Einstein's discovery that everything is energy helped launch a whole new science, Quantum Physics, which states that nothing is really *separate* from anything else, everything is interconnected and interrelated. Quantum physics also concludes that the consciousness of the observer affects the things we observe. Therefore, everything is relative to perception. Quantum reality is very different from Newtonian reality. It is an example of *fourth dimensional* perception and intelligence — it surpasses and embraces Newtonian understanding like a teacher's awareness embraces a young student's. Quantum physics opened up a whole new dimension of awareness.

THE FOURTH DIMENSION

The fourth dimension is a range of intelligence and perception that lifts us beyond the ceiling of the third — with thoughts that are more efficient, caring, and hopeful. This dimension increases your power for growth and change. Lower fourth dimensional awareness allows you to philosophize and ponder new possibilities and start to work on inefficient patterns. You'd consider the importance of positive thinking, but you wouldn't necessarily act on it.

While in the lower fourth dimension, you're trying to work things out and it's still like the yo-yo diet syndrome. Up again, down again. You know you should lose weight, you diet for a few days, then someone offers you ice cream and you eat it. You feel guilty and start over again. In the lower fourth, you continually create new stuff — hurts, pain, guilt — to be cleared away. Recovery can seem like a never-ending process because you aren't getting to the root cause of the problem. The lower fourth involves continually working things out, continually healing, dieting, cleansing, clearing. It goes on, and on, and on. Fortunately, awareness does not stop here.

The higher fourth dimension is where the frequencies of love, care, compassion, forgiveness and inner peace reside. As we sustain these heart frequencies, our consciousness has a smoother, more harmonious flow. We experience more hope, and hope is a powerful fuel to create momentum for positive change and fulfillment. The higher fourth represents a quantum leap in human awareness.

The harmonizing, regenerating frequencies of nature are tuned to higher fourth dimensional frequencies. Nature simply radiates frequencies of peace and harmony without stopping to wonder if it's good enough, or whether people will like it, or even whether people will care for it. It just radiates. The higher fourth holds magic, majesty, wonder and delight and is a level of awareness available to you any time you choose to experience it. When Christ came to Earth, he brought in new perceptions of love and broke through many mindsets of that time. He created and left behind an opening into the fourth dimension. This was a powerful transformation for a society that was largely operating in the second dimension — the undeveloped mind. In the higher fourth dimension you see union, you see all people as one. Christ had a constant clarity of vision, and he loved everyone he saw. His mission was to touch all people and "lifestyles." He mingled with all segments of the population, all the people. In the higher fourth, you don't judge or overcare about someone's lifestyle. You only care about the style and focus of your own love and awareness, and feel true care for all.

The planet is poised to begin operating more consistently in the higher fourth, but it will take a potent infusion of fifth dimensional energy to break free of the density and stress of third dimensional thought. And, it will take people becoming more self-managed through the heart to transform our current thinking habits into higher understandings of love and care.

THE FIFTH DIMENSION

By operating from the heart, you build a bridge of awareness from the third to the higher fourth dimension — a bridge that leads to the inner knowingness of the fifth dimension. In the fifth, awareness is guided by intuitive directives that free you from the endless cleansing and recovery of the fourth, and from the self-limiting fears and phobias of the third.

Fifth dimensional intelligence provides streamlined inner efficiency — for you, me and the entire human race. Stress is transformed through the heart. There are no limits. You are responsible for bringing heaven to earth. You perceive and understand everything as light, energy and frequencies, and it's up to you to manage your energies effectively. Actions are neither good nor bad, right nor wrong, but rather energy-efficient and leading to more love, or less energy-efficient and leading to more stress.

Each new dimension embraces the intelligence and awareness of the perspective below it. In the fifth dimension you comprehend the third and fourth dimensional perspectives without being limited by them or judging them. You understand why people think and act the way they do, even though it may not be efficient or in their best interests. The fifth is a powerful dimension for good, for creative manifestation and self-empowerment. It is the dimension where *you* truly create your own world and are not a victim anymore. From a fifth dimensional perspective, stressful times are seen simply as *untransformed opportunities* for more love and empowerment.

At this time in history, some fifth dimensional energies are filtering into people's awareness. These frequencies are received through intuitive breakthroughs and new technologies that can usher the world past the ceiling of the third dimension. A dimensional shift is emerging.

The great world teachers have said, "God's will is found in the chambers of the heart," and "The kingdom is within." Mohammed said to his followers: "Consult thy heart and thou wilt hear the secret ordinance of God proclaimed by the heart's inward knowledge." As you learn to go to the heart, you discover God's will and your inner will. You gain your freedom. As you learn to listen to your heart directives daily, you can assume the power to manifest them. But, if you ignore your heart, you remain bound in the limits of the third dimension, creating stress for yourself. If you just hear your heart directives, without acting on them, you remain caught in the continual struggle of the lower fourth. Follow your heart — that means following your spirit. Allow yourself the gift of moving on into higher awareness.

It really doesn't take a huge effort to know what your heart is telling you. You don't have to be a genius or even know all the math of the heart. If you spend a little quiet focused time, you can develop your heart intuition and knowingness. As you sincerely go for deeper levels of love, the results you'll have in well-beingness and increased quality of life will motivate you, leading you to wider dimensional awareness. The results are so rewarding you can easily develop a passion for self-management.

A DIMENSIONAL GAME

If you try to understand dimensions from a head perspective, it can be frustrating as the mind runs up against its limitations and mind-sets. So try this as a fun game. This book is written like a dimensional ride through third and lower fourth dimensional descriptions of stress and higher fourth and fifth dimensional descriptions of energy and the power of the heart. Watch how your own energies flow as you read different passages. Try to stay in a higher heart perspective without judging ideas that seem new or strange. Try not to fall into third dimensional anxiety as you recognize areas in yourself that you need to change, or lower fourth dimensional feelings of how much work is needed to transform a long-standing pattern. Treat it all like a dimensional ride. The more you stay in the heart, the more fun and understanding you will gain.

CARE — A DIMENSIONAL PERSPECTIVE

One day I looked up "care" in the dictionary and I was astonished. Care is defined by Webster as suffering of mind, grief; a burdensome sense of responsibility, anxiety; concern, solicitude, and worry. Think about it. None of these descriptions feel good, nor do they sound like fun, peace and harmony. They certainly don't describe the feeling of true care I felt when I first held my newborn child. Webster's definition describes the limiting third dimensional thought patterns of care — or *overcare*. Care in the third dimension is not attractive.

In the fourth dimension, you have the power to be free from overcare, to truly care, and you're more familiar with the qualities of love. Having felt and experienced love quite often, you would *understand* the truth that love is what makes the world go 'round. Your understanding would come from the core heart frequency of love. You would begin to feel the frequency of unconditional love — love without judgment, fear, impatience, resentment, self-pity, worry, sadness. In other words, unconditional love is love that doesn't slip into stressful overcares colored by mind biases. When that happens, your love becomes so colored with qualifiers that it's no longer of significant value. Love can become so coated with negative attitudes from third and lower fourth dimensional energies, that it turns into a deficit instead of an asset to yourself and others. It's important to remember that in the higher fourth dimension you truly *do* feel care about the world, the environment, the educational system, the people, the laws and so forth. But you don't slip into the anxiety of overcare because you know that will drain you and make your caring less effective. True care has wisdom and discernment. It is love in the active modality — the higher heart and mind joined together.

The fifth dimensional thought patterns of care are energy-efficient and on a mission — carrying out your purpose. You realize life is a game you play with your own self. In the fifth dimension, you are creating your own universe, so in truly caring you want to run your system as efficiently as possible. The voice of your heart would be loud and clear; your spirit would be speaking. And if you were waking up to who you are, getting to know your complete self, you would follow your spirit, which is made of light. You would put your knowingness into action, creating as you go. In this dimension of light and love, the universe rearranges itself to accommodate your picture of reality.

THE GLOBAL PARADIGM SHIFT

The more I understood the different dimensions, the more important to me it became to truly care for people. As time went on, my associates and I gained deep insights into the global paradigm shift that is now occurring. I will share some of my perceptions, in hopes that you will read further with more love and care in your own heart.

This is a challenging time in history. The world is going through a global paradigm shift, moving as a whole from the third to the fourth dimension and taking a quantum leap into the edges of the fifth dimension. You can see signs of this in all the rapid political and social changes that are occurring. The end of communism and the fall of the Berlin Wall are just two examples of changes that occurred much more rapidly than third dimensional awareness could have predicted. Mass consciousness tends to move in waves as old patterns and crystallized structures crumble. The pendulum swings into love, back into fear, into love, back into fear, back and forth. An example of this can be seen in the ethnic wars that broke out in Europe after the iron hand of communism was lifted. For months the countries felt great hope, then the violence began.

The problem is that third dimensional frequency perspectives see people, structures — everything — as separate from each other, with tremendous duality, antagonism and opposites. So, in this dimension people gain a little hope, then revert back to fear. There are still thick boundaries and strong limitations in the thinking of the world. Mind-sets are so rigid that when amplified by unmanaged emotions, tremendous conflict results. Third dimensional awareness keeps hitting its head on the ceiling of its own limitations. Because it sees with separate eyes, there are many enemies. If you project into the future and can't see a way out of a dilemma, you can become fearful. When fear is present, the consistency of love cannot hold.

Only the power of the heart can provide the bailout, the higher dimensional understandings. As the dimensional shift takes place, it gives the world a chance to see past old boundaries. It brings a different hope, and a glimpse of new wonder. As the planet moves into faster, higher vibrational frequencies, you, and any person, can take the frequencies available to you in any moment and transmute them within yourself through the heart. You will be presented a new perspective of the world, one in which head and heart are united in clarity. You sustain this perspective as you manage your physical, mental and emotional natures through heart intelligence. Everyone has a heart, and everyone can prosper from using their heart. Such is the power of the dimensional shift occurring on the earth at this time.

As the global transition from the third to the higher fourth dimension continues, more people will become unwilling to participate in actions that do not promote real wholeness and well-being for themselves, their country and their world. Increasingly, people are waking up to the inefficiency of old patterns of thinking and acting. As our social frequency perspective shifts into the fourth dimension, we will establish proven paths to global well-being that do not depend on illusory short-lived attempts that always crumble. Ongoing racial and ethnic conflicts will accelerate mass realization that we need to finally build a foundation of real care and love in our interactions. As a result of global TV and satellite communications, millions are recognizing that antagonism and separation only result in greater despair, stress and planetary distortion. Real peace will come as people decide there's no choice but to make peace within themselves. Following the heart is the key.

OVERCOMING INERTIA

One of the basic resistances to this higher vibration of peace is human inertia. Many people do not consciously value peace enough to bring about inner change. Some avoid trying to achieve balance and fulfillment because they fear failure. But this fear is not based in reality. It's just a projection of the third dimensional limits they've put on themselves. They allow this fear to control them. Heart intelligence helps you understand your fears, then, naturally they dissipate.

In personal and international relationships of the future, *attempts to overpower others* will be seen as dysfunctional behavior. Such actions will be recognized as harmful to global balance and peace. Love is inevitable; it is our true essence. We are multi-dimensional beings waking up to our own higher natures. As we love more, we break through old barriers and crystallized patterns. However, going against the flow of the planet's transition into truer love will create overloads of stress. Resistance to change creates inharmonious feedback in the human system, affecting family, business, social and political structures. This is already happening. Conscious, intelligent love can overcome all resistance. There are solutions, knowledge, understanding, and tools to facilitate. You can make this dimensional shift an adventure. Through the heart, you will have the understanding necessary to be buoyant, strong, clear and courageous through this shifting of the world. Remember, love conquers all.

The power of love, or heart power, is qualified power, based on how well energy is managed within a system. Picture the heart as the hub of a wheel of power; the spokes of the wheel would be its conduits. In an individual, the spokes are the mental, emotional, physical and other aspects of our nature. In a family or organization, the spokes are the collective individuals. What is the United States of America but a collection of individuals? It's the same for a city, a gang, a corporation, the world and, yes, the same principle applies to the universe. The universe is a collection of individual energy units. All parts working harmoniously together create wholeness.

The heart empowerment of YOU — mentally, emotionally, physically — accelerates evolution. It immediately begins to activate your next level of self-growth in the most fun, rewarding, energy-efficient manner. As you love people at deeper levels, you make it easier for them to access these heart frequencies. Through the heart, God's intelligence lifts you and speeds you on to new understanding in the higher dimensions. Stuck in the head without heart contact, the accelerating evolutionary energy only intensifies your inner conflicts and stress. As more people come into deeper contact with the power of the heart, stress will be recognized as an *untransformed opportunity for greater empowerment.* Heart empowerment, not ideally but *actually*, can bring in the intelligence to end the conflicts so prevalent in the third dimensional world. In the higher fourth dimension, all opposites cease to be and all that is seen is the One Light. This is not the end of seeing, but it is the end of seeing with the separate eye. It is *direct perception* that all is energy, not just a *theoretical knowing.* As my Dad, a retired Lieutenant General in the Marines, says when he signs his letters: E Pluribus Unum — "From many, one."

AN AIRPORT STORY

"So, what is this 'hidden power of the heart'?" a business executive asked me one day during a long talk at an airport. Our plane was delayed and he had struck up a conversation while we waited in the lobby. He was concerned about the state of the world, the upcoming presidential elections, and felt we were all victims of the troubled economy. He told me about his stressful job, his recent divorce and his struggles to make ends meet. These problems kept him awake at night and he felt extremely stressed. He didn't believe in religion, but knew there had to be *something* that science would eventually discover to explain what human life was really about. He hoped brain/mind research would find the answer.

In the course of our talk, I shared my perceptions of the heart, that in fact it does contain the hidden power and intelligence that people sense and hope are possible. I told him that personal empowerment is a trend of the '90s because *many people*, like himself, are tired of feeling like victims of life.

He listened. The idea that, scientifically, there might be a "hidden power" in the heart intrigued him — could life really get better? A practical businessman, he asked what tools he could use to access this power. What I told him you will read about in the next few chapters.

Chapter 7

Heart Power Tools

W hat would it be like to have fulfilling feelings of love and care flowing through your system most of the time? If you could buy tools to help you feel more love, would you? What if the instructions that went with the tools were to practice regularly, as you'd do to learn golf, a dance routine or a new video game? Whether your goal is less stress, deeper love, or balance and fulfillment, using even one or two of the heart power tools *consistently* can transform your life.

By activating *the fundamental core heart frequency bands* in your system, the tools connect you with your heart power. Your sensitivity increases, communication becomes clear, understanding develops, and perspective widens. Consistent practice can bring results, often within a few days. Using any one of the tools is profitable and yields high dividends. Try them. You might like them.

These tools are for all people — regardless of age, sex, awareness, race, color or religion. They are gifts for the evolution of mankind. Some of them may sound like "old hat," like you've heard them before — and you have. But they have tremendous power, which has largely gone unused. They draw upon the intelligence of your own heart to activate higher heart frequencies of love, care, compassion, appreciation and forgiveness.

LOVE IS A TOOL

How can love be a tool? To use love as a power tool, simply focus your attention on your heart center, activate your own love for someone and radiate that love frequency. As energy goes out it comes back. As your love goes out it comes back — adding to deeper feelings of love within you and in your interactions with people. As you continue to send out love, the energy returns to you in a regenerating spiral. Your system accumulates the energy of love, just like it accumulates stress. As love accumulates, it keeps your system in balance and harmony. Love is the tool, and more love is the end product.

Love is empowering. Many people who thought they were already loving are astonished at the change they experience when they sincerely use love as a tool. Their comments are almost evangelistic, revealing a new understanding of the regenerative nature of this hidden power of the heart. As they focus their energy in the heart, then radiate love, they are amazed at the new textures of love they experience. The difference between how they felt before using love as a tool, and after, is astounding to them. It feels like coming home. They have more contact with their real spirit. As the Bible describes it, "The fruit of the Spirit is love, joy, peace, patience, gentleness, goodness, faith." (Galatians 5:22)

"Love" is not some sweet, pollyanna, goody-two-shoes frequency band. The words "love," "care," and "appreciation" are like little word cages for wide, powerful energies. As science proves that "love" is an intelligence unto itself, then researchers will more objectively respect its wide range of potentials. Physics has demonstrated that once two particles touch, they have a permanent connection that goes beyond time and space. Studies are already taking place on the effects of love in relationship to healing. Cardiologist Randolph Byrd recently conducted a ten-month scientific study with coronary patients at San Francisco General Hospital on the effects of love and prayer in healing. He applied the most rigid criteria possible for clinical medical studies. The results were remarkable. Significantly fewer drugs and surgical procedures were required for those patients who received conscious love and prayer than for those in the control group who didn't receive this help. According to Larry Dossey, M.D., "If the technique being studied had been a new drug or surgical procedure, it would almost certainly have been heralded as some sort of 'breakthrough'."

There is a difference between consciously directing your life with the energies of love, care and appreciation flowing through your system, and just letting them be there as the mood arises. It's like the difference between using a Makita power drill and a regular screw driver to build a house. As you practice with focused attention, you become much more efficient and knowledgeable in directing these energies. Love is the most powerful core heart frequency of all, and, yes, it is the real hope for the world. Love encompasses all the other power tools and is the first and most important tool.

Practicing the tool of just loving people changed my life. Sometime ago, I read a popular book about how people need to express anger and learn to *fight fair* in order to have a more loving marriage. In trying these techniques, my husband (at the time) and I found a certain release in letting out anger, but it didn't last. Fighting fair got some communication going, but we still had to deal with the depleting effect of anger and judgments. Speaking our truth without the heart was draining. The results were quite different when we began to use the tool of just loving each other while we expressed our feelings about a problem. I practiced sincerely sending love as I spoke, and found that love didn't repress my feelings at all. In fact, by consciously loving, I could more clearly express them. Then I continued to send love while I listened to his response. Our communication was extremely effective. We got to the real issues more quickly. The energy of love created a secure safety zone that enabled us to be less defensive and more honest. It started taking down the fences that previous anger, hurt and fear had erected.

As children, many of us threw temper tantrums to try to get what we wanted. As we grew older, we realized that tantrums didn't work and that both arguments and the "I won't speak to you" cold shoulder routine don't get you very far. I found that conscious love *blows open* the door to real communication and gets me what I really want. You feel so much better inside. So this is where I started building my bottom line — loving the people. How do you do it? You just remember to do it. *Just love the people — any people and all people you meet.* You're doing it for them, but most of all you're doing it for yourself.

Just loving the people, which of course includes yourself, is the bottom line energy equation for ongoing peace and fulfillment. Through loving people, you activate your heart energy which balances your system and brings peace. Heart energy flowing through your feelings, mind and body brings a deep sense of fulfillment. You are *filled-full in love.*

SINCERITY

Have you ever noticed how a *sincere* request from a young child touches your heart? You want to do what he or she asks, even if it means getting down on all fours to play. If children misbehave and then *sincerely* apologize, your heart goes out to them and you can't help but forgive them. Sincerity is a higher heart frequency band that acts like a generator for all the power tools. It has tremendous leverage. Plug into deeper sincerity and you boost the power of whatever tool you use. Sincere love keeps widening your intuition by creating alignment with your higher self. As you love sincerely, you draw in that wider perspective of higher intelligence which gives you more understanding in your relationships, in work and play. Then, if old feelings of anger or hurt arise, your intuition shows you how to release them. *Sincere* love radiates heart power into density where you can effect change. At the same time, it keeps the sense of fulfillment growing and expanding. Real practiced love is what evolution is all about.

LOVE TAKES PRACTICE

For nearly two thousand years people have quoted the Biblical description of love that states,

> "Love is patient; love is kind and envies no one. Love is never boastful, nor conceited, nor rude; never selfish, not quick to take offense. Love keeps no score of wrongs; does not gloat over other men's sins, but delights in the truth. There is nothing love cannot face; there is no limit to its faith, its hope and its endurance. Love will never come to an end." (1 Corinthians 13: 4-8.)

Love is talked about, sung about, philosophized about, but what if love were ever sincerely and seriously practiced?

HeartMath is a system which can help you understand love, how to practice it, and why. Most everyone knows what it feels like to love or be loved in some way. Love is the power that connects and completes. Practicing love is not a new idea, but it's an idea that hasn't been fully understood. Through practicing love, you develop greater awareness and understand more programs from your heart computer that you can implement in life.

Love isn't always soft and gentle. It can be explosive and energizing. It can have a bottom-line, business-like quality to it. Because it connects all, love creates communion, resonance and deeper communication.

Don't confuse love with sympathy, overcare, sentiment, expectation or attachment. I was once very attached to a boyfriend. I thought it was love, and when he started going out with other girls, I felt he didn't care for me and was rejecting my love. I expected him to want only to be with me. Less than a year later I fell in love with another man. When I ran into my former boy-friend in a clothing store, I realized there had been love there but what I'd really felt for him before was mostly attachment, a security blanket which I had confused with love. Real love is so much more powerful than at-tachment, sentiment and expectations. My friend Lew sums it up, "Real love eats all this for breakfast." Real love is caring, forgiving, appreciative, and compassion-ate. It transcends the limitations and fences we create in the name of love. It nourishes, embraces, fulfills and rewards. Through eons of time it's been known and written — love conquers all obstacles.

The first step in the equation for fulfillment, one that everyone can understand and do, is to love people. A real love for people (and not just thinking you love) unfolds as you focus on your heart and practice sin-cerely sending love to whomever you encounter. It's ironic that many people believe they love others, though they rarely do it consciously, except on occasion with a few close friends or family. They know they couldn't sing or play golf well without conscious practice, but they think their love is automatic. Conscious loving il-luminates the heart so that it can function at its full po-tential and act in its intended capacity. The more that people practice real love, the better chance the world has to dissolve its social problems and recreate a soci-ety that can take care of all its people.

In learning how to really love people, it's impor-tant to practice *loving whatever comes your way in life.* Whatever the situation, face it with love. That also in-cludes whatever arises inside you. Whatever negative thoughts or feelings you have, confront them with love.

Connect with your heart computer for deeper under-standing. Keep your energies in your heart and learn to "Love" powerfully all the time. Loving someone is the most magnificent thing you can do for yourself and for them. As you love someone, you dissipate negative en-ergies and bring in understanding.

LOVING YOURSELF

Often loving yourself seems harder to do than lov-ing others. My friend Wendy and I talked about that one day. I explained to her how much easier it is for me to feel love for other people than for myself. Sometimes, when I realize it's time to just love myself, it's hard to feel much love. I feel I'm unworthy or not as talented as I want to be. She experienced the same thing about her-self. We laughed and realized we could both see past other people's shortcomings and love them. We could see their inner beauty and potential. But since we're with ourselves all day long, we're our own worst critics.

People are often most judgmental of themselves. That's because we pay a lot of attention to how we look, how we're doing, where we want to improve, etc. By confronting any uncomfortable thoughts and feelings you have about yourself with love, you will interlock, connect, and balance all the energies in your system. In loving your negatives, you neutralize self-judgments and gain more power to self-correct. Practice keeping your energies in the heart. That will help you activate feeling frequencies to find the flow of love. Then you can build on it. You can use imagery to help. Sometimes I imagine my heart is a waterfall flowing through my whole being; sometimes a flute blowing heart energy to whatever I'm loving; sometimes a well — I prime the pump for a few moments until it flows on its own.

Practicing the heart power tools means keeping your energies in your heart to get that feeling of love going. It means reminding yourself throughout the day to sincerely love — people, yourself, your family, your job, nature — Life. Your power builds as you learn to love at deeper and more sincere levels. Watch how the energy of the heart rounds off the rough edges inside you.

Love is not limited to just religion. Love *IS*. It can add to whatever religion you're in or path you're on. Love facilitates any system. All that my friends and I did at the Institute was to research what could facilitate people's happiness. We wanted to find what would be a booster pack to real fulfillment. What we found were power tools for the people business — the biggest business of all. Fulfillment isn't something that ends or stays at a plateau. Empowered by real love, fulfillment completes at each level and goes on.

Chapter 8

Tools for Rapid Self-Adjustment

A s you reap the rewards of loving yourself and others, you will become motivated to build your heart power to love more consistently. The Heart Lock-in is a potent tool you can use anytime you want to contact a deeper heart frequency. It can be a refreshing break from the head and, with a little practice, feels good, activates your heart power, and helps you maintain better balance.

THE HEART LOCK-IN TECHNIQUE

You start by finding a comfortable place to sit, closing your eyes and relaxing. To Lock-in, shift your attention from your head to your heart, by relaxing your thoughts and focusing your energies in the heart area. Then send a sincere feeling of love or appreciation to yourself and others. Just love people. Appreciate the good things in life. Appreciate your life compared to tougher situations, like people who are homeless or starving. This helps facilitate the deepening of heart resonance. Just let go of mind chatter and release your feelings in the heart. If head thoughts come in, bring your focus gently back to the heart area and radiate feelings of love and appreciation.

If you can't feel love right away, or if you feel some pain in your heart, it's okay. Try to tune into a memory of when you loved someone and it was easy, or a time when you deeply appreciated someone and there was no insecurity or anxiety. Focus on that clean higher heart feeling. Then your love will have a higher quality.

If you've had a combination of lower heart and head creating insecurity and vulnerable feelings in your life, these feelings often are stored in your unconscious. With practice, the Heart Lock-in can release them and take you to a deeper heart security. Security is what finally transforms pain and old hurts. As love increases in quality, the old attitudes of expectation and attachment release bit by bit. View all of your feelings that arise in a Heart Lock-in as love that is growing but is not yet completed in its highest quality.

Experiments show that when people close their eyes, they tend to let their focus go to the head, which can stimulate the thinking process and inner dialogue. So in a Heart Lock-in, you focus your energies in the heart area, not in the mind, forehead or solar plexus. Remember, the main intention of a Heart Lock-in is to experience your own heart more deeply. If draining thoughts come in, look at them objectively and go to your heart computer for understanding and release. Be consistent, but be casual in practicing your lock-ins, then they will flow. If you try too hard from the head, you create mental tension that blocks your higher dimensional awareness. Take five minutes or more during your day to feel love in your heart for yourself, everyone and everything around you. Try to find a peaceful, still feeling and a warmth around your heart center. The more you practice, the easier it will be to feel a deeper heart contact.

Music can be effective for enriching a Heart Lock-in. There are many types of music that help to activate heart frequencies. Music has the power to change the mental and emotional atmosphere in a room and to change our moods. Think about how the different kinds of music, rock, country, classical or jazz, each create different feelings inside you. I like to listen to music called *Heart Zones** when I lock-in. *Heart Zones* was designed by Doc Lew Childre to connect people with their heart power, and to reduce mental fatigue and emotional burnout. Doc spent several years studying and testing musical tones, harmonic resonances, inverted rhythms and specific chords for their effects on psychological stress patterns. Sophisticated testing of EEG (brain) and EKG (heart) frequencies showed significant changes in a very high number of people. To me, *Heart Zones* is like a fun buoyant tonic or attitude refresher for the mental and emotional nature. One newspaper article described it as a "musical cup of coffee without the edges" because it gives many people a focused, energetic clarity. I've used it in my lock-ins for a long time and it's become a good friend — a friend that creates a good heart feeling.

* Available from Planetary Publications. See page 273.

DEVELOPING INTUITION — THE WHOLE PACKAGE

Everyone has flashes of intuition, but intuition only develops as you learn to listen to and act on your heart's directives. One aspect of the HeartMath system, called Intui-Technology™, researches the inner technology of intuitive development. It offers advanced methods for stress dissipation and the systematic unfoldment of intuition. Intui-Technology brings in wide fifth dimensional awareness to facilitate new breakthroughs in business, medicine, science, politics, social affairs and economics.

The occasional flash of intuition that most of us experience is useful, but it is only a piece of the pie. Wider intuitive bands that can benefit you, the nation, and the world, are accessed through the receiving station of the heart. As more people make that one effort — the practice of contacting the natural intelligence of the heart — they will realize what a bailout it is for the world, though not an instant one. The ratio of energy return for your effort is 1:9 — one effort yields a nine-fold return. This is because the heart has a multiplier effect: It is designed to look after and take care of your entire system. Such is the hidden power of the heart. It functions in numbers of power, like the equation $E=mc^2$. The higher fourth and fifth dimensional energies accessed by the heart have tremendous transformational power.

You can tune in to the "intuition station" — your heart is the control knob. Using the heart power tools helps you stay tuned to the station. Without the bottom line of heart development, you won't be able to hold the frequency and will keep getting off track, even if you access some isolated frequencies of intuition. As increasing numbers of people develop their heart intelligence over the next ten years, we will see a quantum change in the way "intuition" is experienced and understood. As our political leaders develop intuition, they will work with *everyone's* needs in mind. They will see that it's short-sighted and inefficient to please only isolated interests. "Intui-Technologists" will be the planetary stress-busters with the power to create positive change that will encompass the whole world.

FREEZE-FRAME — AN INTUI-TECHNIQUE

Here's a technique you can use anytime, whether you're working, driving the car, talking to someone or watching TV. It has been extremely valuable in my practice of heart development.

To Freeze-Frame you stop the movie of your life for just a moment and go to your heart as the director. It's especially helpful if you're having a problem, because it helps you relax and detach from your mental or emotional identification with the issue. This is a good first step in gaining objectivity. When you become objective, you can choose the most efficient course of action. It's like pushing the pause button on your VCR. You are actually stopping your holographic movie — so you can re-create your own reality in the moment. You focus your energies, stop the movie — still frame (like taking a snap shot) — then go to your heart computer for direction. The next frequencies you choose will activate the next program, the next scene in your movie. Remember, you are creating your own movie by your perceptions and choices in that moment. You do have choice, and all your little choices really do count. At any moment, you can go to the heart and change the frequency.

Have you seen the Holodeck on board the Enterprise in the TV series *Star Trek: The Next Generation*? The Holodeck is a life-like 3-D hologram. The crew asks the master computer on the Holodeck to create any setting, experience or situation they want. And that's what they get, complete with everything their imagination would desire. They walk right in and participate in the holographic movie, and it all seems totally real. They can freeze the hologram at any time and instruct the computer to change the program. Practicing Freeze-Frame helps you re-create your own movie of life in the moment by accessing a new program from your heart computer. And *your* movie is totally real.

With Freeze-Frame you create a momentary pause so you can just be still and collect yourself in the heart. Calm your head chatter and emotional reactions, then shift the energies to the heart. It takes practice, but the practice has a big return. Freeze-Framing gives you a break from inefficient mental and emotional reactions. Then you can choose to self-adjust, saving energy and building power in your system — your own power.

Freeze-Framing works better when you *remember* to activate a positive heart frequency. As you put your movie on pause, make a sincere effort to feel something in your heart, such as love, care or compassion. This sets the stage for your heart intuition to come in. It's no different than fine-tuning your radio dial to get a clear station and tuning out the static. You may not always be able to feel a deeper heart feeling right away, but stay focused in the heart. The sincerity of your effort can reconnect you to your heart current and start the juices flowing. To plug in, think of someone you love or remember what feels good, maybe a fulfilling experience. Feelings help you remember. You become sensitive to the difference between head reactions and heart feelings — they really do feel different. Remembering this difference helps you go back to the heart more often — it feels better.

If you're practicing Freeze-Frame in the middle of an emotional reaction, try first to *neutralize* the emotion. As you focus your attention away from the problem and activate your heart power, it's easier to quiet your inner noise and feel calm. As Erin, a 13 year-old at the Institute says, "Chill out!" Then your intuition can deliver a wider understanding of the situation and a release. Practicing Freeze-Frame has improved my intuitional capacity and given me a joyous sense of freedom, self-security and self-esteem.

Heart intuition is a feeling of knowingness. It comes in quickly with a little practice. But don't be concerned if you don't get clear answers right away. Some situations don't have clear-cut solutions and take time to work out. After some practice, you learn to sit back and watch your life geometries unfold to bring you solutions. Freeze-Frame is a fantastic power tool for cutting through stress; it just takes practice to verify how the process works in your own system.

Freeze-Frame is so simple and so practical that you can use it moment-to-moment to prevent stress while you are on the move. It's one of those handy "all-in one" tools that helps you contact your heart, balance your energies, release or prevent stress, and gain intuitive solutions. You will find that you become more sensitive to your emotional, mental and intuitive natures. You can also use the Freeze-Frame technique anytime you want creative inspiration or deeper intuition on a subject. Remember, the mind works most creatively and efficiently when it engages the heart.

FREEZE-FRAMING A THOUGHT LOOP

Thought patterns are those "random dialogues" or "inner soundtracks" of your perceptions of life. As you observe them, you'll see they tend to run in loops. We've discussed how some of the most common thought loops are repetitive patterns of worry, anxiety, fear, resentment and unfulfilled desires. They keep you on that inner (and not very fun) merry-go-round. Sometimes multiple thought loops run continuously without resolution. Here's a Freeze-Frame game to try when you want to quit replaying stressful tapes like, "I should have said this," or "I should have done that." Thought loops like these used to keep me upset all day, and constantly bleed my energy.

When you get caught up in a thought loop, Freeze-Frame and say to yourself, "Oops, no big deal," and don't self-judge or analyze. As simplistic as this may sound, when sincerely applied it's a potent heart tool. It helps you look at yourself like a child learning to walk. You wouldn't beat a child for falling down or stumbling as he was learning his first steps. You'd say, "Oops, no big deal." That creates a heart frequency of care, compassion and forgiveness for the child so he can learn faster. You can do the same thing for yourself to help bypass thought loops. You'll grow faster because it keeps the learning process lighter and fun. Hiking up a mountain is a lot more fun when you take off your backpack. Don't judge yourself if you stumble or get tired, just move on to the heart and you'll get stronger. "Oops, no big deal" teaches you to self-adjust without self-judging. It's like a stepping-stone back to your heart. It gently shifts the energy, opening the way for intuitive understanding and release. Each time a thought loop comes up, remember to Freeze-Frame, say "Oops, no big deal," go to the heart, let the patterns go, then move on. This technique will build your self-management muscle — it soon gets easier and more automatic.

Each time you make a self-adjustment, you add energy to your system. That's the fifth dimensional perspective. Self-judgments and self-beating block energy. They inhibit action and drain you. Self-beating is part of the blindness of the third and lower fourth dimensions, creating tremendous stress and disease in people. As you practice the Heart Lock-in, Freeze-Frame and "Oops, no big deal," you become sensitive to your inner truth. When the mind is slowed down, your heart intuition manifests more fully in your awareness. Watch how you can eliminate fears, anxieties and resentments! You'll soon be able to recognize the real intuitive voice of your heart and consciously move to a higher dimensional perspective.

MORE GAMES TO SWITCH OFF UNWANTED HEAD FREQUENCIES

So what do you do when your mind processes through a complete negative thought or even a whole stream of them? Here's a game to try. As soon as you recognize the negative thoughts, switch frequencies and end that unwanted thought with a sincere, positive thought. Nurture the positive thought with good heart feelings for a moment. Then, end that positive thought with a "period" at the end of the sentence. Let it all go, move on, and continue with your day. This is not just a mental attitude adjustment, which can be repression. It's heart power applied to the times when you are caught in head loops and need a transforming tool to *remember* to shift to the heart feelings and regain a positive perspective. Each time you do this you build your inner security. And security is power.

Here's another game I use: Take time during the day to say, "All right, I'll think only positive thoughts for the next five minutes" (or longer if you like). As a negative thought tries to pop in (they almost always will), you just say, "Quiet — this is my heart time for positive thoughts." I try to stop the negative head processor at the beginning, on the first or second word. It's actually fun to practice "being positive" with heart power. Remember, the true addictions in life are your thought patterns. Whatever your mind feels you have to have in life for your peace is a clue to what you're addicted to. It's okay to be addicted to love, balance and fulfillment. It's actually real smart. They all feel good and don't have any negative side effects.

As I practiced these games, I saw that increasingly my heart was running the show. What resulted was an amazing number of efficient solutions. I received intuition on problems, on creativity, on diet, on managing my time, and the list didn't stop. If I ever felt run down,

I could find the inner peace I needed and easily recharge through the heart. As I developed a more sincere heart in myself, I also found a deeper inner balance.

DEEP HEART LISTENING

Freeze-Frame taught me how to listen more deeply to other people's hearts as well my own. I practiced what we call "Deep Heart Listening" by focusing the energy in my heart while I listened to someone talk. I learned to hear their being, their essence speak. At first, I noticed that while I was trying to listen I would run subtle head tapes of my opinion — whether I agreed or disagreed, how I would have handled the situation, and so on.

Try not to listen with the head. Nine times out of ten I'd find myself doing that. As I practiced loving and deep heart listening, a miracle happened. I experienced a wider perspective of my consciousness which led to a more sensitive, essence-based understanding of what the other person was really trying to say. There was a real heart connection with the other person's heart. I found that making that connection plugged me into a current, and it took less effort to keep it going. I had a deep realization that people are not our enemies; they are our friends. They all have hearts, even if they often perceive things differently. My mind had known the truth of this before, but to have that intuitional light bulb turned on and directly *feel* it was truly enlightening.

When we don't deep heart listen to people, we can make a lot of assumptions. For example, when a co-worker from another department used to borrow my pens, stapler, scissors and other supplies from my desk and never return them, it infuriated me. "How many times do I have to remind him? He doesn't care about me — he has no respect at all or else he would return them." I felt justified being upset and stressed out about it. I talked to him several times, but nothing changed. He was oblivious to the problem and that made me even angrier. My heart directives showed me how my irritation and resentment were creating a stress feedback loop. Even if it was his fault, getting stressed about it was *my* fault. I intuited I should keep myself in balance, appreciate his positive qualities, and then talk with him. Once again we discussed my feelings about people borrowing my supplies, but this time I felt a heart connection, and he really seemed to hear me deeply. I deeply listened to his response and realized that regardless of whether he changed or not, he was my friend and did care. I was able to totally drop the resentment and we made an agreement I'd remind him if he forgot, which he did. But after a few reminders, he always remembered. Magically, the more I deep heart listened both to myself and others, the smoother all situations worked out in life. But, if I didn't listen to my heart directives, I'd always regret it later and have to deal with the consequences.

DEEPER LEVELS OF FREEZE-FRAME

You might ask, "Well by now, why wouldn't you listen to your heart directives?" Sometimes I'd have little whisper thoughts, one liner thoughts, or seemingly *justified* thoughts and I'd doubt or forget my heart directives. Life would then swiftly give me feedback in the form of stress. So my next effort was to actually focus on my head and check out these justified thoughts. I'd let my head talk, with my heart surrendered to it. The heart would just listen and give it understanding. With Freeze-Frame, I could step back and listen to myself from the heart's perspective. At times, I was surprised to see myself caught up in a head program that I wouldn't have noticed if I hadn't started checking. I began to notice all sorts of subtle head chatter that I wasn't aware of before. Yes, I had many thoughts that seemed totally justified. My head would think it was okay to analyze, process and ponder a situation. It would say, "I've got to figure this situation out!" But then the head would jam, and in would roll the mist and the fog. Before I knew it, finding the solution to the problem would turn into those same old thought loops again. I would run into ceilings and walls in my inner rooms, like a trapped bird trying to find its way outside. So back to the heart I would go, training my mind to let go, realizing that heart intelligence would let me again know the most efficient solution.

Learning to trust your heart is a process that unfolds as you explore the inner workings of your head and heart. The head is designed to think, analyze and figure. So use your head programs to get the facts and issues clear. Once you've done that, *but before you start processing*, take all that data into your heart computer. Hold it there for a few moments and find your peace and balance. Freeze-Frame in the heart, love yourself and others, and the solution will find you. That creates a smooth interface between the head subterminal and the heart computer. Try this for yourself and see.

To develop your intuition even further, go for deeper levels of Freeze-Frame. I like to Freeze-Frame and then love for increasingly longer periods of time. I set the time in advance. First I started with one minute, then two, then five. I increased my heart focus power to even go for ten minutes without any thoughts. I'd Freeze-Frame for ten minutes, then send out love for ten minutes, then release the mind and go about my day. An hour later, I'd play the game again. As your Freeze-Frame practice deepens, it's fun to watch a thought impulse come up but never really form into a thought. Remember, it is inefficient to judge yourself if your focus slips back into the head. Just try to stay in your deep heart intuition for longer and longer periods. As I played this game, I found on some days it was easy while on other days it was a real challenge, like stretching new muscles, especially if something happened that bothered me just before the time I'd set aside for the game.

ONE-LINER THOUGHTS

Through this process I noticed I had a tendency for what I call "one-liners." I would greet someone and before I knew it thoughts like "she looks good" or "he seems a little out of sorts" would pop up. In other words, one line assessments. If another person's energy made me feel uneasy, I'd make an assessment that could turn into a judgment, such as, "Something's wrong with this picture." It didn't matter whether it was a person I knew, the color of a car, or the anchorwoman on the evening news — one-liners would accompany whatever my head took in as data. I wondered if it was possible to take in perceptions without the one-liners that categorized them either on the good list or the bad list. I recognized one-liners as a standard old third and fourth dimensional thought process. It was a major insight to realize what a fine line there is between simple assessment and judgment. One-liners were robbing me of the opportunity to see everything in a fresh new way, as a child would.

So I created another fun game to consciously observe myself as I approached each situation in life. It was an important fine-tuning game for operating from the heart at a deeper, more sincere level. Try this game. I call it "On Your Toes." Whether you're balancing your checkbook, greeting a person, talking on the phone, editing a paper, or any other activity, consciously watch for one-liners, Freeze-Frame them in the heart and notice any new intuitional perceptions. I was amazed how much fun this added to my life. I was learning how to truly live in the spirit, in the higher fourth dimension. Intuitive perceptions feel so good to the human system that you want to keep Freeze-Framing your head into your heart and wait for that direct perception. It keeps your childlike spirit alive.

WHISPER THOUGHTS

Energy follows thoughts. Whatever thoughts you think, that's where your energy goes. As your awareness develops, you realize it's simply not energy-efficient to have inefficient thoughts. I began to look at what I call whisper thoughts, the seemingly quiet ones you barely notice. Did they also take away from being in the moment? I noticed I had soft whispers that ran continuously throughout the day. I whispered about my day, what to do, what not to forget. The list seemed endless. Only after I practiced Freeze-Frame for a while did I realize the whispers were an energy leak. Please understand that I'm not saying whisper thoughts, one-liners, thinking, analyzing, etc., are negative frequencies. But, if you let them run constantly, it's like a faucet with a slow drip. Self-empowerment is a fun process that comes from being conscious of how you're managing *all* the energies inside you.

As I developed my heart intelligence, my intuition would come in at the appropriate time so I didn't have to keep circulating the same list of reminders in my head. At times my intuition would tell me to write down a thought on my "to do" list and get it out of my head. I realized that some of those whisper thoughts were helpful but some were just nagging insecure thoughts about what I needed to do. As I released many of them, I experienced a new level of intuitive organization. Many people write "to-do" lists, but there are also the lists of whisper *feelings* that don't quit. As you develop your intuition through Freeze-Frame you start to notice your multi-level inner processes. You become sensitive to the whisper thoughts and feelings that are energy-draining. I came to view them as a constant noise in the background that slowly wears you down.

So what can be done to keep your intuition running all through your day, without the draining whisper thoughts? Here's what I did. Many days when I woke up in the morning my mind would start to list all the things I had to do that day — phone calls, letters to answer, household responsibilities, normal everyday stuff. I would diligently use my daily planner to organize my priorities, then sit down for a Heart Lock-in. That's when I'd notice the whisper thoughts start: "Don't forget to..." Each time they came up, I would ask my heart for deeper understanding. My heart told me to just let them melt away, that everything would get taken care of...just let go into a deeper level of peace and silence. The inner silence felt so good. As I practiced this, the power of my heart began to grow more and, magically, everything that really needed to get done did, and right on time. I intuitively knew what to do when, and my work days would flow just right.

All my associates at the Institute use the Freeze-Frame games and although we manage five businesses, give seminars all over the country and have many visitors, our days flow in creative harmony with little stress or strain. We love to share with others how we have learned to empower the heart of business. It all starts with loving people and loving yourself, doing Heart Lock-ins, using these simple Freeze-Frame techniques and following your intuitive heart directives.

Chapter 9

Speak your Truth:
Honest Communication

Deep listening from the heart is one half of true communication. Speaking from the heart is the other half. They are like two sides of a coin. *When you remember how you like to be spoken to*, that helps you speak from your heart and helps the other person listen better. We have a motto at the Institute, "Communicate as you go, don't wait 'til you blow." I've become very aware that when I don't speak my truth, and let things build up, I feel terrible.

A friend and co-worker tended to be irresponsible. He was in charge of warehousing and receiving. Occasionally he'd neglect to notify the store clerks that an important shipment had arrived. It didn't cause a major problem so I let it go. But I still felt irritated. Not long after one of these incidents, he was supposed to run an errand for me and forgot. I felt frustrated and knew I should talk to him but I didn't make the time.

Then we passed each other in the hallway as I was rushing to meet a deadline and he started telling me about a silly problem. I got angry inside and judged him for being insensitive. Later, I felt some guilt that I hadn't yet talked to him.

When I heard he was complaining that I didn't have time for him, I was stunned. I had all my reasons, but suddenly they seemed flimsy. I felt disappointed and hurt. The next time I saw him, he brushed past me. I felt squashed and resentful. I went back to my desk totally numb and about to blow up. My unsaid feelings were piled up inside me. I Freeze-Framed and went back to my heart, realizing I'd done this to myself by not speaking with him along the way. My heart had quietly tried to tell me several times, "Please speak your truth from the heart. Use your discretion, but talk to him."

I had to really ask myself, "Why didn't I speak my truth?" This was only one situation out of several where I didn't speak up. I could see it was a pattern. I was receiving tremendous inner feedback from several areas in my life, creating piles of stress. Then a pile would crumble from over-stacking it on the inside. Without release, depression would soon follow.

I'm not naturally aggressive or outgoing; I'm on the sensitive side and usually fairly quiet. For years one of the biggest deficits on my energy balance sheet had been my reluctance to communicate in the moment. I had a list of reasons for not speaking my truth which seemed valid but were not. Underneath I was just scared and didn't know why. Finally, I was determined to get to the bottom of it.

In many heart discussions with myself, I went over

the reasons I found for not speaking in the moment. The list read like this: "I don't want to offend someone," "I don't want to interrupt and be rude." "They probably won't like what I have to say or like me for saying it." "It will just turn into an argument." Another good one was, "No one gave me a chance to speak, so they probably weren't interested in what I had to say." No matter what reason I gave myself for not speaking up, I'd feel frustrated. Then I'd tell myself, "I can handle my own feelings, no one really needs to know." It seemed easier this way, until a pile of these unresolved feelings came crashing down on me. I had to ask myself, "Were all my reasons just coming from my ego? Could I be fooling myself?" After all, I didn't think other people were stupid for speaking their truth from the heart. No, I thought they had courage.

If you find you're not speaking the truth, access your heart for the reason. Are you just scared and don't know why? Heart intelligence can help you overcome insecurities by giving you clarity and understanding. With pen and paper, you can heart-map a solution. Ask your heart for the steps to start speaking your truth. Your heart can tell you when speaking your truth would be energy-efficient or not and advise you on the best timing. It can turn any deficit into an asset. The heart is not about right and wrong. The heart is like a friend who wants to help you reach understanding whether it's with yourself or others.

Not long ago, I wanted to tell a good friend that her non-stop, rapid-fire talking irritated me. But I didn't, and she kept on doing it. I was feeling like a victim of intimidation. My fuse got shorter. I went to my heart and asked why I still hadn't said anything. I had to consider, was it due to head frequencies, like fear of rejection, desire for approval, or avoiding an argument? Or, was it due to heart intuition telling me to be sensitive, get more clarity, or wait for better timing? In being honest with myself, I saw that it was a mixture. I finally decided the most efficient thing to do was to be vulnerable and have the courage to speak my truth. I did. I spoke from the heart and we probably had the best talk we've ever had.

Being vulnerable doesn't have to be threatening. Just have the courage to be sincere, open and honest. This opens the door to deeper communication all around. It creates self-empowerment and the kind of connections with others we all want in life. Speaking from the heart frees us from the secrets that burden us. These secrets are what make us sick or fearful. Speaking truth helps you get clarity on your real heart directives.

The combination of speaking my truth and deep heart listening is one of the best gifts I've found in life. It's taught me I can be myself, my whole self. What an elated feeling to finally understand something about myself that's been like a tree limb blocking a panoramic view! When you sincerely want to know what another person has to say, you receive more power to deep heart listen which opens wide the windows of perception. Real communication is from the heart. Deep heart listening and speaking your truth generates an exhilarating "heart talk" frequency. "Heart talk" is care in action and builds friendship. As you learn to see everyone as your friend, and not as an enemy, you release judgments. Just keep your heart open to them as you speak your truth.

There will always be people with whom you feel more resonance than others. There will also be people with whom you don't feel any resonance at all. You can still love them without judgment. Tune into their essence. That's one of the serious practices of self-empowerment — to be in the heart and love people, whether or not there's a resonance. Practice sending love and care whenever irritations or judgments come up — on the bus, at work, at home, anywhere. You can learn to love anyone when you activate your heart power and go that extra mile. You don't have to agree with them. You just build tolerance and compassion for every type of person you meet. Christ and other great teachers had that kind of compassion, especially for those whom others might reject or judge. Real heart empowerment would have to be about that.

Chapter 10

Releasing
Judgments

How you perceive life — people, places and things — is of the utmost importance. There is such a fine line between assessing a situation and judging it. Assessments, when not made from the heart, often become judgments. Judging oneself and others is such a mechanical habit, a commonly accepted frequency in our society. But it generates a tremendous amount of stress. In using the word judgment, I'm not talking about the ability to discriminate. I'm talking about the judgmentalness that comes from mind-sets or insecurities that color your perceptions and affect your ability to discriminate truth. You are hurting yourself if you don't give yourself a wider perception of a situation by taking the data objectively to your heart, and then using your heart intelligence to make a clear assessment.

Most people don't consider themselves judgmental, they "just know" things about people and issues.

The mind receives data and compares it with what it already "knows" to decide its perception on a subject. I had to ask myself if this "knowing" was from opinions or from true heart intelligence. Judgments are often subtle, formed from old hurts, pressures, stress, haste, and comparisons between yourself and others. Comparisons are tricky. It's extremely easy for a comparative assessment to turn into a judgment. As Doc Lew Childre says in *The How To Book of Teen Self Discovery**:

> "Understand that everyone has their own path to follow in life that is unique and different from anyone else's. Don't judge or envy anyone else's shoes. Just learn to get the most out of the ones on your feet. It cuts stress."

Teach yourself to make heart assessments. Recognize a quality or character trait in someone, but if you disagree with it, don't judge them, just love them to find understanding. Try to see what it's like to be in their shoes. Your heart frequencies could help their behavior improve, and you won't be adding more stress by judging them. Give people the latitude to be themselves. You would want someone to give that to you. I remember when people used to judge me as being hyper-sensitive and overly emotional. Since I was already feeling insecure, their judgments could make me feel even worse. At other times, people would judge me for keeping too much to myself and not communicating. Often they were right. If I was insecure, I'd freeze inside and be unable to speak. But sometimes when I was quiet, it was because I was considering the best way to respond. When I felt wrongfully judged, I'd get angry. I was trying to find my balance in communicating and it seemed

---

* Available from Planetary Publications. See page 274.

like I'd be judged no matter what I did.

People naturally have a desire to find balance in their lives. Often, what we judge others for is where we ourselves lack balance. You can't always know what another person's life is like. One time I judged someone for being inconsiderate. He was supposed to meet me at a stoplight at 3:45 and drive me to a repair shop. I was looking forward to a chance to chat with him, hoping to catch up on news of his children who were friends of my son. I waited more than twenty minutes in the pouring rain. It was almost 4:15 when he finally got there and he didn't offer any explanation nor did he apologize for being late. I thought he was terribly inconsiderate. "Surely, if he cared about me at all he'd say something," I thought. He didn't, so I didn't say anything either. He asked about my family. I responded curtly, "Everyone's fine." At home, I told my husband how disgusted I was. I'd never ask a favor of him again. The next day I discovered his secretary had written the time down wrong and he had no idea I'd been waiting in the rain. I had incorrectly assessed the situation and now I felt like a heel. While I was relieved to be free of the judgment I'd made about him, I felt sad that I'd jumped to conclusions and missed a chance to really talk.

Judgments block you from connecting with the essence of another person. They create imbalance and disharmony in your system. As justified as they can seem, I've never known judgments to ever help anyone. When you assess someone or something, watch your next thoughts. That's where a judgment can come in. If you go past the line, then you get into judgmental energy which feeds back on you. It doesn't feel good to you or to the other person. Judgments create an inefficient feedback loop inside, especially when your perception is charged with negative emotional energy. Not only does judgment effectively stop the flow of heart energy and real communication, it destroys relationships.

If you're the one judging someone, you are draining your energy. You pay the price, not the other person. People and life are always changing, so judgments often limit your perceptions and stop your next level of knowingness. When "you know what you know," you put ceilings on the capacity to expand and experience the new.

A friend of mine told me about the first time she'd ridden a horse in twenty-five years. She went with experienced riders up some beautiful mountain trails. She felt awkward. The saddle hurt and she wasn't really sure what she was doing. She judged the other riders because they were not considering her situation. When they started to gallop, she knew she didn't have to. But, in the excitement, her horse took off too. Head thoughts came crashing in, saying, "Make the horse stop!" "You'll fall off!" "Your butt is really going to hurt tomorrow!" "You idiot!" But as she relaxed and went with the flow, her heart began to burst with joy — she knew she needn't stop that horse. They rode for hours and a feeling of exhilaration stayed with her through the next day, sore bottom and all.

Don't many situations that look one way at first, and then change, become add-ons to your life? If you would let your inner child perceive someone or something first, you would be more open to discovery. Looking through the eyes of a child, life has a wonderment to it and becomes fun. You are in charge of your perceptions, so you can choose either to judge or be open. One drains energy, the other accumulates energy. Judgments create separation and alienation, openness leads to connectedness. Whichever attitude you choose, that's how your life will be.

For example, let's say you're at a party and you see someone whom you immediately dislike because of the way he looks, something he says, the way he carries himself, whatever. Later, you get to know him and you become good friends. A lot of people have this experience. They often laugh and tell others how they didn't like each other at first. The sad part is all the fun and quality in life many of us miss because of an initial judgment.

You can't live in this world without some assessments. But be especially aware of emotionally charged assessments that become justified judgments. Judgments leave a residue, a residue called stress.

"JUST LOVE THEM"

If you are dealing with fears and insecurities from old head programs, have compassion for yourself. Just love your insecurities, fears and resentments. Release and forgive them as they come up. Judging, beating, or repressing insecurities just gives them power. Then you have a pattern that never gets resolved. Recognize that your real security is built from your relationship with your own heart. Insecure feelings used to give me so much pain that I'd judge myself for them, repress the feelings so I couldn't feel the stress anymore, and feel unlovable. But I would love someone else if I knew they were doing this to themselves. It was a real revelation to have compassion and heart for myself. That's when I started to release those insecure feelings. When you just love your insecurities and use your heart intelligence, you learn to understand and make peace with them. They go away! "Just love them" is an inside tip at the race track.

There is a cloud of judgment and insecurity frequencies hanging over the world. It's a major cause of global stress. Judgments of yourself or others are comparisons between how something appears and how you think it should be. I felt stressed and I thought I shouldn't be that way, so I got angry with myself. I thought I should feel happy but I wasn't and got annoyed. These comparisons led me right down the garden path to self-judgment.

What are self-judgments? They are those head processors: "I'm too fat, skinny, clumsy, dumb, I did wrong, I blew it, I'm not efficient, effective, or good enough." Self-judgment can drain you as fast as judging others. Self-judgment destroys the feeling of connection with your heart, your source of power. You cut yourself off from your power when you judge yourself. It's like cutting your own throat. Self-judgment depletes you and often isn't even a correct perspective.

For example, you could start out by judging yourself for being too slow or unskilled in one small aspect of your job. Next, you're beating yourself for not doing better in several other areas. You start to feel like a failure and bemoan the fact that you are in the wrong job or were never given a fair chance. If you had gone to your heart computer when the first judgment came up, you might have come up with a more self-appreciative perspective and a creative solution.

A healthy critique of oneself, with compassion and care, is beneficial. It leads to self-adjustment. But if you notice self-judgment creep in, practice Freeze-Framing. Care that you tried to do your best. If you need to change, then attempt to, but don't beat up on yourself. If you do judge yourself, admit the inefficiency, and self-correct. No big deal. Just go to your heart and see the wider perspective. That gives you the energy to really understand and change!

Chapter 11

Inner Security
Your Key to Self-Esteem

A s Doc said in a talk one night, "Self-esteem is the amplified essence of heart power. It's the energy your system generates as you gain confidence in yourself." Self-confidence is based on your true level of inner security. You build inner security by trusting in your heart, clearing out old head programs and learning to follow your heart directives. Inner security is like coming home. As the wise old saying goes, "Home is where the heart is." Inner security and self-esteem are by-products of managing your energies from your heart, which releases powerful energy into your system.

In the third dimensional perceptions of self-esteem, people try to *get* self-esteem in different areas. They look for confirmation from "outside" to tell them whether they have self-esteem. People acquire self-esteem in isolated areas — such as physical fitness, sales success, becoming a movie star, etc. Look at a scholar who wins a "Who's Who" award, or a talented salesman who wins the trophy for highest sales volume. They each shine with self-esteem in that one area. But at home, the salesman may have an alcohol problem, a poor relationship with his wife, or be abusive with his children. The scholar may have many secret insecurities. Well-rounded or complete self-esteem is the result of building well-rounded inner security and heart empowerment. That comes from having more assets than deficits in your energy account at the end of a week, month, or year. Self-esteem energy accumulates in your system and helps release old problems and old thought patterns. You feel free, limitless, and capable of doing anything. Then spirit rushes through your system.

Real self-esteem is really the spirit manifesting through your entire system. It's far more powerful than the current third and lower fourth dimensional concepts of self-esteem. Heart power is what releases real self-esteem. It's generated from the securities you have built in the heart.

Inner security is like fire power for self-esteem. Becoming secure in the heart builds powerful energy accumulators which magnetize all the aspects of complete self-esteem, like personal magnetism, charisma and other leadership qualities. It creates a life of balance and fulfillment — and a feeling of being at home wherever you are.

Chapter 12

Uncovering Compassion

C ompassion is care with passion. Passion is a neutral energy that adds to and amplifies your care. When you care and have a passion to understand and help others, you have compassion. You can see passionate care in the Mother Theresa's of the world. Something burns inside their hearts in endless service to the sick, the destitute and those whom society has forgotten. You can see compassion in the eyes of a kind teacher, whose heart goes out to a troubled child. You can find it in a wise judge who looks deep into the heart of the accused with a clarity that transcends the letter of the law.

Compassion digs for the quality of deep understanding. Isn't our judicial system founded on the premise that all are innocent until proven guilty? That's the bottom line of compassion, although many forget it in the heat of today's social problems. Unless you love people, you can never understand them. When you love enough to put yourself in someone else's shoes, you discover compassion. True love and compassion release other people to be themselves because they finally feel understood. Care and compassion are heart frequencies that are activated by a sincere attitude of wanting to help. They are power tools that, if used, strengthen your connection with your own heart and your ability to love.

Quite often compassion slips into the lower heart band of sympathy. Sympathy drains your energy and bleeds you of your vitality because it has qualities of sadness, pity and remorse. Using your heart intelligence, you can walk in someone else's shoes without walking off the cliff with them. You have respect for both yourself and the other. Sincerely loving them creates a new perspective of balanced understanding.

FEAR

What people often perceive as the evil and difficult side of human nature is laced with what most call *fear*. I choose to call it a lack of understanding. Many times when something is new or unknown, and you don't understand the situation, it can create fear. In a stressful world, people instinctively respond from the head, with frequencies of anger, paranoia or defensiveness — all forms of fear. Fear is an illusion of the mind, yet all fears have a "make-sense" to them. There is always an answer and a satisfying understanding that releases fear, even if it isn't at your fingertips in the moment. Your heart intelligence can release you from fear if you give it a chance to bring in a new perspective. But if you're locked into fear, the mind doesn't see any way out.

Fear is an unpleasant emotion caused by anticipation that something bad is going to happen. Fear of the unknown comes from not being able to perceive life from the heart. We fear we will not be able to understand and adapt to change. Usually, we like change if we can control it — knowing what's coming, moving at our own speed, etc. But life doesn't tend to deliver like that.

Fear can be paralyzing. In inner cities, like Detroit, New York and Los Angeles, a majority of people live in fear — fear of leaving home at night, fear of drive-by shootings, fear of rape, robbery and other violence. In suburbia, many live in fear of losing their jobs, of a lowered standard of living, or fear that the violence of the city will spread to their neighborhood.

Fear is also created by the memory of having experienced hurt, pain, sadness, or anger, and not wanting to experience it again. You may be protecting those places in your heart that were bruised. If you glaze over your fears pretending they don't exist, you are still harming yourself. Science has shown that repressed fear secretes hormones in your bloodstream that have a debilitating effect on your immune system. Compassion for yourself is a powerful tool to release those fears.

Quite often, an open heart results in feeling the pain of humiliation. You probably had times in life when you loved with the openness of a child, then someone treated you without compassion, laughed, or even punished you for being that way. So you closed your heart out of fear, to protect yourself from ever feeling that pain again.

Fear is a deeply rooted frequency in our stressful world today. People build emotional defenses and then deny their feelings. Fear gets buried under layers of denial, often turning into repressed anger and hostility. The suppression of emotions is unhealthy. When your anger has no place to go, it can turn into an attack on yourself, or it can generate blame for others and result in an unjustified attack on them. To release your anger, first try to love or feel compassion for those you want to blame. This can help you calm down. Then try to share your anger with them without an attack. Express how you feel without blaming them for making you feel that way. If you turn rage outward in blame, it will kill your relationships; if you turn rage inward, it will kill you with disease. Unexpressed anger and rage eat away at you like a cancer, while hostility and venting anger often lead to heart disease.

At an annual meeting of the American Heart Association, several papers were presented on the effects of anger and hostility on the heart. The SAN FRANCISCO CHRONICLE reported,

> "For years, many experts assumed that hard-driving, impatient people with classic Type A personalities were at high risk of heart attacks. But many now believe that the truly lethal personality trait is hostility and anger.... When people get angry, their bodies pump out stress hormones, such as adrenaline, which trigger the body to release fat into the bloodstream to provide energy. People with high hostility at age 19 tend to have high cholesterol levels at 40."

It is neither possible nor desirable to avoid all painful and sorrowful experiences in your life. They help you deepen your feelings of compassion for yourself and others. What you need to do is take conscious responsibility for how you choose to perceive painful experiences. You can make your decision from the third dimensional head perspective or from the higher fourth dimensional intelligence of the heart. Fear-based decisions made by individuals in the name of self-protection, are what created the limiting perceptions of separate races, cultures and nations. Individuals who break these patterns of history will lead us through the passageways of compassion and understanding and into the consciousness of self-empowerment.

As the world steadily turns back to the rights of individuals and individual responsibility, it will also have to honor the principles of the collective whole. In God's plan, everyone would be taken care of, so there would have to be compassion for all. The shortest route to the heart of the matter is to "love," taking personal responsibility for using your higher intelligence, your heart computer. *The fundamental change for the world will occur when we as individuals open our minds to heart perspectives.*

ARE WE VICTIMS?

"I'm Dysfunctional, You're Dysfunctional," is the title of a new book pointing out how America has become a nation of victims. It's a trend to blame our parents for our dysfunctional behavior. When I was in college and just starting out on my own, I blamed my parents for having sheltered me too much. I had only lived on military bases and entering mainstream society was a shock. My parents diligently followed all the disciplined rules of the base. Like many young people tasting independence for the first time, it was convenient to blame anything I didn't like about myself on them. Watching my college friends do the same thing, it didn't take me long to realize that no matter what my upbringing (or perhaps because of my upbringing), I was responsible for myself. Today, I sincerely thank my parents for how they raised me and the example they set for me. I value self-discipline and the core values I learned.

In this stressful society, there is so much we all have to cope with, it's easy to blame our problems on others. "Codependency" is a popular term today, applied to any problem associated with any addiction, real or imagined, that involves another person. In exploring codependency, many are trying to reclaim a sense of identity, power, and balance so that they can stop feeling victimized in their own lives. It is easy to feel discouraged with ourselves and that discouragement leads to more self-judgment because we feel we "should know better" and "should have learned by now." It may very well be true that dysfunctional families are incubators of shame, guilt, anger, denial and self-doubt. It's not a child's fault for having adapted dysfunctionally to a distressed family environment. But it is an adult's responsibility to release the blame and take on the self-work that will reshape their adult experience. Many continue to see themselves as adult victims of early family dynamics rather than as self-determining participants.

The victim scenario repeats itself in towns and cities all over our nation and is a trend of our larger cultural environment, regardless of race, religion or socioeconomic status. We realize there are problems, but don't know what to do about them. We fear dying young, but fear growing old. We fear not finding the right relationship, but fear we've found the right relationship. Here comes marriage, and we fear being tied down. We fear not getting a new home, but fear the stress of house payments and upkeep. Nowadays we yell, scream and hate ourselves — internally beating ourselves up. What we do to ourselves is oftentimes worse than what we blame our parents for. Usually, we don't think to feel compassion for our families having done the best they knew how. Somewhere along the line we are accountable for ourselves.

Emotional energy turned inwards is our own personal self-created hell — illness, violent relationships, drug addiction, alcoholism, child abuse, compulsive eating, anorexia, depression and obsessions are the grim results. Yes, we pass our attitudes on to our children. The collective hell turned outwards creates violence, gangs, crime, homelessness, war and starvation. Is our disease, individually and socially, an addiction to negativity and pain?

GRIEF

With all our pain, we retreat behind the prison many of us have erected around our hearts for self-protection. But we haven't imprisoned anything but our pain. Grief is the iron bars that surround a heart in pain. As the mind plays tapes of grief, the real heart seems very distant. Grief is a state of mind that has turned its back on the power of love. It manifests as a deep feeling of being unloved. To live in grief is to live in loneliness, cut off from the gift of life.

Sometimes life presents situations that cause a painful shock to your system—bankruptcy, job loss, divorce, betrayal, death of a close friend. Grief occurs when you allow that shock to consume you. The mind keeps replaying the painful experience again and again, building the power of despair as it goes. For example, when a loved one dies, you feel loss and sorrow. As we acknowledge and focus on the sorrow, grief results. But the tendency of the mind is to hold onto grief. Society encourages it. If you're not grieving enough over the loss of your husband or wife, society judges you. If you're not crying enough at the funeral, you think people are looking at you disrespectfully.

The mind recoils at losing what it holds most dear. The tendency of the mind to hold onto guilt and fear, to cling to self-judgment and blame, is an aspect of grief. We become rigid with denial and self-protection, and sink into a feeling of "not enoughness." Inside, we look into a warped mirror, created by the inharmonious frequencies of third dimensional thinking. Our self-image seems distorted, unacceptable, unwhole and unlovable. Our thoughts tell us we are unworthy and useless. What a living hell we have created for ourselves. Yet, we hold on — our grief has become a stimulus that gives at least some deeper feeling to life.

People often say they drink excessively to block the pain of grief. But often, it's just a launching pad for further exploration of despair. They become pitiful so they can feel the anguish at a deeper level. Why this fascination with despair? It's because people have not learned how to re-connect with their heart power after a painful event has short-circuited the connection. To feel deep grief is better than not to feel at all.

Through the intelligence of your heart, you can release the self-victimization paradigm that bleeds and drains the quality of life. The darkness of the helplessness and hopelessness can be illuminated by the heart, in a clear and merciful awareness. What seemed so untouchable is reclaimable with the power of compassion. The iron bars begin to melt. When heart contact is finally reestablished, it changes your perception. Through a deep willingness to surrender to hope, you can let go of grief and allow your heart to speak.

Some are able to release grief far more quickly than others. However long it takes, it is always the re-connection with the power of the heart that moves you past grief. When the heart is enlivened again, it feels like the sun coming out after a week of rainy days. There is hope in the heart that chases the clouds away. Hope is a higher heart frequency, and as you begin to re-connect with your heart, hope is waiting to show you new possibilities and arrest the downward spiral of grief and loneliness. It becomes a matter of how soon you want the sun to shine. Listening to the still small voice in your heart will make hope into a reality.

FROM RECOVERY TO DISCOVERY

The first step in recovery, whether from grief or any addiction, is to realize your heart is your power source to help you stop this *self-abuse*. Many recovery programs require you to admit that you are powerless and to submit to the authority of another. God would like us to use our "heart intelligence" and discover ourselves. Recovery is only half of the healing process. Acknowledging that you are powerless, unmanageable and addicted is a first step. But don't stop there, keep growing. With a deep willingness to surrender, you can let go, listen to your "still small voice," and allow your unhappy life to change.

Self-pity can be replaced with compassion for yourself and others. It is compassion, rather than self-pity, which makes the greatest contribution to true growth in recovery. While some can acknowledge that "others have suffered more than I," not many people are able to sustain that feeling of truly "counting their blessings." Sooner or later most people find themselves on the "pity pot." The 12 Steps program tells the newcomer not to worry; they only have to change one thing – everything! Without inner heart management, this kind of effort and change in recovery is extraordinarily difficult. Very often, the lack of inner balance leads to simply changing addictions, then coping with new addictive behaviors.

"Recovering, never recovered" is living in a state of fear that addictive behavior will again control your life. Recovery is not complete until you move beyond fear and realize that we can and do recover. True and lasting recovery is achieved by developing security and understanding within your own heart. Heart management allows you to transcend fear, transform addictive behavior and literally erase such patterns from your system. Heart security enables you to move beyond "recovery" into a new dimension of life experience — *discovery*.

All of us have some kind of grief to explore. Grief of incompletion. Grief of not having what we wish. Grief of shame. Grief of humiliation. Grief can be loss of control, death of friends or loved ones, even the loss of one's pet. We ask, "What did I do wrong?" "Why did this happen to me?" It is the feeling of separation from ourselves and others to which the word "grief" can most accurately be applied. Real grief is the separation from your heart.

For example, when I was a teenager my best friend in the world was my horse, Shaquita. Every day I'd ride alone in the jungles and on the beach in Panama, where my father was stationed in the military. I loved her more than anything. When my father was transferred back to the States, I knew it was impractical to take Shaquita with me. I felt like I'd lost everything. There was an empty space inside. I couldn't imagine how I could ever fall in love with anyone or anything as much as my horse. It was many years before I realized that it was my own heart opening that had felt so wonderful. That experience, as painful as it was, gave me a depth of feeling that opened a new chapter in my life. My only true desire was to feel that love again. In my search for love, I came to deep understandings.

Falling in love is magnetic. Our hearts open and we become extremely receptive. We're more flexible and life has new sparkle. Some people fall in love with God and it feels even stronger than falling in love with a person. A mother falls in love with her child in a different way, but feels it just as deeply. All are aspects of the open heart, ready to receive. It's the open heart that people yearn for to bring them fulfillment. In looking for love, we are looking for more of our own heart. When we lose the object of our love, the loss of that part of our heart can seem unbearable. When we try to go back to the heart and feel our love again, the old pain comes right with it.

The heart can feel like it hurts too much at times to want to put your energy there and feel what the heart feels. But it's the pain of the heart shut off that hurts the most. You feel you've had to cut off a flow of love to a person or thing that is no longer there. Don't get caught in a cycle of blaming and cutting off, blaming and cutting off. You'll only prolong your pain. I discovered that there are plenty of people around to love, including myself. Try feeling compassion for yourself. Be gentle and kind inside as you reach for understanding. That will release the pain and let you feel your love again.

You'll discover that real love is millions of miles past falling in love with anyone or anything. When you make that one effort to feel compassion instead of blame or self-blame, the heart opens again and continues opening. It's only a mind-set (but a strong one) that says you need to have a certain something to feel that special feeling in your heart. Life will bring that feeling back to you, but you have to be open — it may come gift-wrapped in a different package than before. Your spirit wants more than anything for you to feel that total fulfillment, without dependency on someone or something for your security.

When you think another person is responsible for your happiness, then your lower heart bands of attachment are involved. Attachment keeps you bound to insecurity. It's not that you didn't love. You did. But it's the mixture of love and attachment that's confusing. You can tell you're in lower heart bands by the way they drag you around. The deeper heart builds inner security and that is what finally transforms the pain.

Whether you're in a relationship — with a mate, a

friend, a child — or are alone, you still have a relationship with every person you meet. You have a relationship with your own heart, your spirit, yourself. If you consciously go to your heart with compassion, you will find heart intelligent answers to any relationship issue. Victimhood reflects a collective sense of resignation in our society. It isn't that suffering and loss shouldn't be recognized. If we valued self-responsibility, we would treat victims with compassion and respect but not reverence. So often, friends sympathize and emotionally identify with each other's problems, thinking they're having a heart-to-heart talk. Sympathy is two people crying in their beer, two pitiful people instead of one. This only amps up the emotions which feed the victimizing head thoughts. Then people take actions out of indignation, because of the principle of the matter, and create more stress. Offer compassionate understanding, not sympathy, to friends in distress, then you can help them see from a new perspective. If you cry with them, you give your power to them and victimize yourself.

THE POOR ME'S

You can speak your truth from the heart and stop being a victim of your emotions. Befriend yourself, learn to love yourself enough to stop replaying the same old victim movies. Your inner security, your heart power, doesn't need to be dependent on anyone else, on what they say or do or don't do. Feeling misunderstood, taken advantage of, not getting the proper credit — those times in life when someone or something has done you wrong and you feel justified in getting out of your heart — can be summed up as "the poor me's." Science is proving daily that self-victimization really does affect health. In streetsense terms: People can jog five miles a day and seem in good health, but if they're processing "poor me's" over some problem while they jog, they are releasing debilitating hormones that deplete their immune system. You are the one victimizing yourself. "Poor me" mental processing can ruin your entire day.

Most people find their biggest unfulfillment is in the company of their own self. You can go on a vacation in the woods and just being with yourself can bring more feelings of unfulfillment than the job or home you wanted to escape. The real victimization is needing to have something outside yourself for fulfillment, to fill the "hole in the soul." That's the root cause of all dependency and addiction, trying to fill that hole. Addiction doesn't work. It only temporarily masks the pain and never fulfills that part of ourself. Addictions often cost people everything — family, job, home, self-respect. The pain finally gets too much to bear and the isolation too intense. It usually takes hitting bottom for people to reach out for help in recovery.

EMPOWERMENT

When a person starts in recovery, they often feel an uplift at first, like they're floating on a pink cloud about to be rescued from all their despair and pain. Without learning to manage the self from the heart, the new high doesn't last. People revert to self-abuse again. The real process of recovery would involve four stages. The first is admitting you're in addiction. This requires self-honesty. The second would be uncovering what took you there. Many get stuck in a loop at this stage, identifying with the old hurts over and over again. You can never build self-esteem through constantly victimizing yourself with the old hurts. Be willing to cut your losses and self-empower here; then your third stage would be to recover to balance. Without balance you can't enter the fourth stage: Discovering your next level of fulfillment and fun and sharing that with others.

Many times you might feel despair about your recovery process and wonder if returning to your addiction wouldn't be better than experiencing the difficulties of your life. You might let your head run in its own loop about what is not right in your world, adding emotional intensity to your feelings of despair. You weigh out the pro's and con's of drinking or using something or someone again. Then you judge yourself for even thinking about it and feel worse for not being "beyond this yet." You become afraid and anxious that you may not be able to prevent yourself from a relapse.

This is one of those times to know there is a difference between the head and the heart and to practice using heart power tools. Here are the steps. Recognize that you are in inefficient head loops and Freeze-Frame the thoughts of "lack" in your life. Activate compassion for yourself as someone who is trying hard to grow in your recovery. It helps to realize that everyone has some life geometry in which they too could use more heart empowerment. Freeze-Frame your head bands about the details of your issue, and go to the heart computer for a read-out on which heart tools could best help. Then sincerely practice the tool your intuition gives you. Make an effort.

It's important to appreciate yourself and your situation, remembering that things could always be worse. Recognize that you are experiencing the effects of old patterns of thinking and feeling that drain your power. Keep Freeze-Framing these thoughts as they surface. These steps are all acts of loving yourself. Love, love, love yourself, but don't turn around too quickly to see if the flower you've planted in your heart yesterday is growing yet. Soon your heart intelligence will let you know what's next for you to do. Talk to a friend to help you get a better perspective. Don't be afraid. Your heart will tell you if what they say is right for you.

In the lower fourth dimension, people are recovering, slipping back and recovering. In the higher fourth and fifth dimensions people are discovering. Whatever your grief, whatever your addiction, using the heart tools will give you the power to move from "always working it out" to "being there." As you practice listening to and following your heart, your love will increase in quality, and expectations and attachments will release bit by bit. Use the tool with the bottom line: just love. You know how good compassion feels when you receive it from others. So give it. And don't forget compassion for yourself.

Begin to perceive any problem as an untransformed opportunity for empowerment. Understand that you basically have two choices. One victimizes and ages you, the other empowers you. Soon you will find yourself helping others dissipate their stress through the heart — with a lot of compassion and understanding. In loving others, you help them bypass steps that you had to go through. You awaken your own heart bands and theirs. Everyone doesn't have to go through all the same things. That's what love is, making it easier for others. Watch the hidden power of the heart unfold in our social structures over the next few years as more people catch on to its transforming quality and the opportunity now available.

Chapter 13

The Power of Surrender

W hen you have compassion and surrender to your own heart, you are surrendering to the hidden power in your heart, God. You are surrendering to love, because God is Love, the cohesive force of the universe that connects us all. Surrender is not just a religious concept; it's a power tool for listening to the voice of your spirit and following its directions. When you surrender your head to your heart, you allow your heart to give you a wider, higher intelligence perspective. Remember the phrase, "The real teacher is within you." Very simply, that teacher is to be found in the common sense of your own heart.

To find the real meaning and power of surrender, practice releasing and letting go — just loving. This is not a giving up. Surrender is a process of stilling and emptying the mind. We ask ourselves to shift focus and go to a more understanding perception. That means quieting the head bands for a while and using your heart computer. It means letting go of self-limiting third and lower fourth dimensional perspectives to allow your own higher dimensional awareness to be activated. As you practice this, you will learn to see the divinity in everyone's heart, learning and growing like you.

Surrender is giving up our attachment to how we think things ought to work — the outcome of a situation. It means letting go of the crystallized thought patterns, mind-sets and box-ins that leave no room for a wider perspective. Growth never stops, no matter who you are or how aware you may be. When the mind sets up a temporary truth, and you are sure you know what you know, you don't leave any room for a higher truth to come to you. Leave the box open, give your heart a chance to breathe. Then it can show you new possibilities for fulfillment. New truths will feel good to you once you have gotten the mind-sets out of the way.

Children *know* that they *don't* know, so they are wide open and receptive. They naturally ask an older or wiser person to explain their perspective to them. "I don't know" can be a tremendously empowering statement, especially if you take it to your heart with a sincere surrender to whatever your next step might be. It creates an openness to discovery that can keep the child-like spirit alive.

ENTHUSIASTIC SURRENDER

Surrender is having the intelligence to ask God for an understanding perception of the whole, a new view of a situation. It's easy to do this if you don't care much about the issue or if you're not attached to the outcome.

Then enthusiasm for the surrender comes readily. But the more important the issue is to you, the more important it is to surrender, at least to get a fresh perspective. When there is attachment to the result, we tend to have a hard time giving up control. Let go, enthusiastically surrender to the God in you and the God in others. Love yourself and others in balance. If you notice you are swimming against the current, surrender and flow with the universal current. Consistently follow your heart directives and love. Then, what you're really saying inside is, "I'll manage my energies as efficiently as I can, using my God intelligence." That is loving God. And God is Love.

Surrender helps you to love whatever comes your way in life and stay empowered. From my experience, life is full of the gifts of learning and growing. Some gifts feel quite terrific, so surrender is just a matter of opening without fear to an experience you might have thought to be impossible. If an experience feels unpleasant or painful, true surrender would give you the eyes of the heart to see the gift of growth and embrace it. You can soften and smooth out the jarring feeling of the unexpected with loving surrender.

Surrender is a serious part of your awakening process. It involves truly taking care of yourself and the whole. My friend Wendy began to blossom in unexpected ways when she lost her executive job and became "just a worker." Her branch of a clothing company had been struggling financially. She loved her company and the people she worked with, so she was out there pounding the pavement for sales herself, trying everything she could think of. When the company finally closed her branch down, she felt humiliated. Now the dreams she'd had for turning "her little empire" around were down the drain. All the people in her department were offered jobs painting designs on silk in another part of the building.

Because she loved the people, Wendy went to paint silk down the hall. She kicked and screamed inside at first, angry with upper management. But when she went deeper into her heart, she could see they were doing the best they could for the whole and that their decision had been wise. She realized that they had actually given her more time than most companies would have done to make a go of an ailing profit center. When she went even deeper into her heart, she appreciated she had a job and discovered a delight in her new work. She found herself in a large open room with a group of women she already loved. They laughed and talked across tables where they applied colors to silk that sparkled in the sunlight. Wendy realized this new job was the fulfillment of a secret dream she'd had for many years — to work with her hands in a kind of quilting bee environment with friends who loved her. Out of the rat race of her executive job, she became kinder, more secure, and more fulfilled.

When we know love matters more than anything, and we know that nothing else *really* matters, we move into the state of surrender. Surrender does not diminish our power, it enhances it. Surrender is not giving power way, it is actually joining power. It is the synergy of all your powers, not a weakening but a powerful strengthening inside you. Surrender releases the charisma of the spirit, an invisible energy with visible effects. You become of the moment. You come into possession of your greatest asset for changing the world: *your capacity to change your perspective about the world.*

Enthusiasm created from the heart is the spirit of the matter. It ignites your whole system so there's no drag, no resistance, no thoughts like "Do I have to?" coming from the head to sabotage the power of your surrender. If you are trying to re-create your life and are not excited about what you're creating, then what you choose will not happen. With enthusiasm, you would have the flexibility to sincerely surrender in the moment, to let go, and just love — a true, sincere moment of surrender where only love matters. Ask your heart to help you change something on the inside of you first, not on the outside. Then put your heart into it. That's where lasting change of any kind has to start.

The cure for the people problems of our world is surrender, meaning just loving each other. Children have flexibility and love and surrender more easily than adults, who seem to endlessly attach themselves to the results of a matter. If the ambition of all people was to love (rather than make this amount of money, achieve that result, and on and on), their lives would unfold in harmony from the core. You can't *take* fulfillment. In the heart, fulfillment finds you.

Consider your own life — how many times a day does some situation pop up that leads to moments of frustration and anxiety? Surrendering your head to your heart in those moments will lead you to balance and fulfillment. As you listen to your spirit, peace follows. So follow your spirit. Build your foundation in your heart. Love must be your innermost and spontaneous response towards every person you encounter. Say to yourself inside, "I just love." Use these words as a key to start the engine running in your heart and watch life brighten with new love and understanding. Surrender to your new awareness and let love unfold the purpose of creation to you.

Chapter 14

God's Creation

As the transition into the next dimension of awareness speeds up, more pieces of the puzzle can fall into place for everyone. Long awaited answers on the process of creation are emerging through DNA research, breakthroughs in physics and new understandings of holography. For years, physicists debated whether the universe started with a "Big Bang" or in some other way. Scientific evidence indicates there was a Big Bang, when all matter exploded from one single point of energy, but the question of whether this was a random event or an act of conscious intelligence (God) had not yet been scientifically determined. Until April 23, 1992, science would not venture past the point of saying the Big Bang was a random event, that matter formed itself out of chaos. Then something happened.

It was interesting timing. I was getting ready to write this chapter when a friend from New York faxed us an article about a scientific breakthrough. Astronomers released new data from the most powerfully sensitive microwave telescope ever built, which was aboard a NASA Cosmic Background Explorer (COBE) satellite. They saw what had never been seen before. It was considered by many astrophysicists as "the breakthrough of the century." Astrophysicist George Smoot of the Lawrence Berkeley Laboratory, announced that he and his associates discovered what they believed to be the edge of the Universe. When scientists view stars in the sky, they are actually seeing them as they were many light years ago. It takes thousands and millions of years for starlight to travel to the earth. Through the new telescope, they saw distant, wispy clouds or ripples of matter that were relics of how the universe looked 15 billion years ago! These ripples were uniformly spread out in the newborn universe and may have started clumping together to produce stars. There was intelligent order present, leading to the mathematical conclusion that: Intelligent intention was present at the beginning of creation. This discovery was far past what scientists had previously observed. According to a statement given by Stephen Hawking of Cambridge University, who ranks with Albert Einstein as one of the preeminent theorists of the century, "It is the discovery of the century, if not of all time." As a scientific breakthrough it brings physics closer to religion, since every religion believes that the heavens and earth were formed by intelligent divine intervention, not by random events.

The LOS ANGELES TIMES reported, "The most miraculous thing is happening. The physicists are getting down to the nitty-gritty...and the last thing they ever expected to be happening is happening. God is showing through." Some Christians say, "These momentous findings supporting the Big Bang theory of creation may confirm that the universe is the work of a majestic guiding hand, providing a common ground for two old antagonists — religion and science." According to physicist Michael Turner of the University of Chicago, "They have found the Holy Grail of cosmology." Harvard astronomer Owen Gingerich sums it up, "Science's essential framework, that everything sprang forth from that blinding flash, bears a striking resonance with those succinct words of Genesis 1:3, 'And God said, Let there be light.'"

Theories of human evolution and the creation of the universe can be completely unraveled as your higher intelligence evolves. Let's take a deeper look at the most popular, current views on creation and evolution. As of today, the three most commonly discussed theories are: 1) the strict Creationist theory, 2) the Darwinian theory, and 3) the Big Bang theory. Most religions believe in Creationist theories. The Judeo-Christian Creationist theory is based on the Biblical interpretation that man was created by God about 10,000 years ago as an act of Divine Intervention. Judeo-Christian Creationists believe that Adam and Eve were literally the first humans and that God created the universe, galaxies, stars, planets and earth, including all animals and plants, as they are, as an act of divine will. Creationist theory does not accept the theory of evolution. Nearly half the people in the USA accept the Creationist theory, at least as it's applied to man. In a 1991 Gallup Poll, 47% of those polled said God created man as a one-time event pretty much as he is now sometime in the last 10,000 years.

I was curious. How did it all begin? How did I begin? Who created me and why? I could understand the Creationists' feeling that every living thing must be a special creation of God. It seems hard to imagine that we evolved from stardust. I studied the current theories, taking each one to my heart computer to gain more understanding. I knew there had to be a way to bring together the more personal theories of creation and the facts of science.

UNDERSTANDING EVOLUTION

The Darwinian theory of evolution is based on scientific evidence that everything on earth evolved from a single-cell organism. This cell divided, multiplied, adapted to its environment and mutated over long periods of time. The stronger organisms continued to evolve while the weaker ones died out. Some evolved into multi-celled water organisms, which evolved into fish, reptiles, lower mammals that walked on four feet, apes that walked on two feet, and finally humans. Darwinian theory does not say how the single-cell organism got there in the first place. The same 1991 Gallup Poll indicated that 40% of those polled believed that humans did develop over millions of years of evolution, but God guided the process.

The Big Bang theory states that all energy (and therefore all creation) started from a singularity. Most scientists now accept that the universe started with a Big Bang, a tremendously powerful explosion of energy from which all stars and everything was created and then evolved over billions of years. As scientists verified Einsteinian equations which mathematically showed a singularity, the Big Bang theory gained strong support. Astronomers have spent years searching for hard evidence to support this controversial theory. The recent discovery by George Smoot is the first time that relics of that original Big Bang have been observed. "As a result," reported the LOS ANGELES TIMES, "theorists have come to the remarkable conclusion that all of the matter in the universe — and all of the space as well — was initially contained in an infinitely dense ball smaller than the period at the end of a sentence." "That may be difficult to comprehend," says Lawrence Berkeley Laboratory astrophysicist Rich Muller, "but cosmologists, like the queen in *Through the Looking Glass*, have to believe six impossible things before breakfast."

Just as Darwinian theory doesn't say how the first microscopic organism got here, the Big Bang theory doesn't say how that original point of energy got here either. In the 1991 Gallup poll, only 9% believed that man evolved by random event without God. A total of 87% believed that God was involved in creation in one way or another. Many accept a combination theory that embraces God's involvement along with the scientific discoveries of Darwin and the Big Bang.

So how do we verify for ourselves which theories, if any, are true? Using your heart computer, you can attempt the exploration of any idea. As ideas (or frequencies) enter your consciousness, your heart computer can intuitively unfold their truth to you, bringing an understanding of evolution. All too often the head comes in and says, "Oh, no you don't! You can't prove it so you must not accept what cannot be demonstrated to the earthly mind and senses."

I find exploring theories is fun. Every challenge in life is an opportunity to evolve. You can meet that challenge by taking it into your heart computer for direction and understanding. You can allow your intuition, directed by your heart, to take precedence over the earthly mind, the head. Let your higher intelligence rule your lower mind; let it rule your life and all happenings in life. It's enlightening to illuminate your lower mind and gain direct knowing. The Bible says, "For as a man thinketh in his heart, so is he." (Proverbs 23:7) If you think with the mind in the heart, you are continually with God. Heart intelligence has the power to order and unfold your template of life efficiently, in universal accord with the Creator.

Our world is rapidly entering a new dimensional template of consciousness that is bringing us back into resonance with the primal Creator. Naturally, there will be some lumps and bumps as our perspectives adjust. This new consciousness is not the historical, traditional human perspective of God. These views are limited by the mind-sets of second and third dimensional awareness — all that people could grasp at the time. Higher dimensional perceptions know God as an omniscient presence or being, having infinite awareness, understanding, and insight. God's being and intelligence resides within all currents of the Universe.

This is the age of your awakening, the time when your heart and head can harmoniously integrate in wider understanding. It's an awakening to the fact that you are responsible for yourself. The kingdom of heaven is within you. Evolution is, sincerely, the ongoing unfolding process of loving and understanding all there is.

SELF-HELP

During the twentieth century, and especially since 1960, thousands of different self-help practices have appeared and been tried by millions. How well they work depends on the quality of the techniques and the sincerity of your practice. "Self-help" would require self-understanding, and eventually lead to an understanding of your whole self. I've practiced many different self-help techniques over the past fifteen years. I feel like I took in the cream essence of each one, and they all led me back to the heart. Only when I began to practice living from the heart, did my life start to change and evolve dramatically.

The difference between how I was fifteen years ago and how I am now is like night and day. Even my physical body has changed. I never thought I could lose weight around my pear-shaped thighs because of the way I was built. Now I am very slender and my facial structure appears different. I used to be passive and slow in my movements. Now, I am highly active and quick. Emotionally, I was hyper-sensitive, uncommunicative and often insecure. I lived a lot in a "poor-me, no one understands me" attitude. I didn't really like people all that much. Now, I am secure, enjoy expressing myself and live in a state of appreciation of how truly wonderful life is. To a large degree, I've balanced my personality and understand myself. I have many wonderful friendships now and really love people, all people.

To me, self-help means we can truly help ourselves by becoming responsible for our head and heart choices. As we do this, evolution rapidly unfolds past what our minds alone can imagine. In my own development, I've achieved a point of head/heart integration which allows me to probe the mysteries of the universe with heart intelligence.

The puzzle of creation has always deeply intrigued me. As I pondered it in my heart, I realized from a higher fourth dimensional perspective that creation and evolution are really one and the same. They are two pieces of the puzzle that only look separate to the lower dimensional mind. As I assimilated data from my heart computer on these two aspects of life, I saw how creation and evolution, together, form the whole. The following few chapters describe what I discovered.

Chapter 15

Holographic Awareness

W ith the same inner perception that I see human energy fields and auras, I also see divine patterns which function as templates for the holographic images in the heart crystals. These templates appear to be influenced and molded by cosmic energy fields. There is some type of weaving factor that seems to unite and fuse different frequencies so they function as a whole unit. I realized as people make choices, they activate different frequencies that come together and form holographic "filmstrips" of their life.

When I first saw holographic filmstrips of seemingly past, present, and future events, I often wondered if the future is frozen and completely predetermined, or if it can be changed. If the future is a hologram for which every detail is prerecorded and fixed, then we are all just acting out a play of our destiny. We would be moving mindlessly through a script that had already been written. If this were true, it would mean there is no free will or choice.

PRECOGNITION

I studied many documented reports of people who had precognitive glimpses of their future. As a result of these glimpses, they were often able to avoid disaster. I read one account of a woman who was about to board a plane. But, as she looked around, all the people who were going to board seemed gray and ghostlike. She had a feeling of doom and chose not to get on the plane. The plane crashed on take-off, killing everyone on board. A close friend told me a story about the evening he and four fraternity buddies had decided to go to a local bar. When they got in the car, my friend suddenly felt in his heart he shouldn't go. He stayed back without really knowing why. That night he was awakened by the Dean of Men who told him his buddies had been in a serious car crash. Three were killed and the fourth critically injured.

The Bible is full of stories about people who received visions or forewarnings, acted on them and changed the future as a result. Noah saved his family and the animals by heeding the warning to build an ark. Joseph was warned in a dream to flee with Mary and Jesus to Egypt, as Herod was going to kill the child. I wondered why precognition wasn't more common in modern times, and realized that, when unbalanced, it easily leads to superstitious beliefs. The development of head logic would tend to dismiss precognitive glimpses as mere superstition, throwing the baby out with the bath water. When balanced with heart understanding, the precognitive ability brings true wisdom.

Recently, I read accounts of identical twins, who though separated at birth, ended up with amazingly similar lives. When they finally met each other, they found they'd married people with the same first name, given their children the same name, had similar careers, owned the same kind of dog, and even wore clothes of the same type and color. There are many true stories of identical twins in which one twin intuitively knows what's happened or going to happen to the other twin. Whenever they can, they warn each other and are able to avoid unpleasant events.

Examples like the above would seem to indicate that there is a fairly detailed DNA blueprint of our future. Dr. David Loye, a clinical psychologist and former faculty member of the Princeton and UCLA medical schools, spent the last two decades investigating precognition. From his findings, he concludes that, "reality *is* a giant hologram, and in it the past, present and future are indeed fixed, at least up to a certain point."

In his book, *The Holographic Universe**, Michael Talbot theorizes that, "the future of any given holographic universe is predetermined, and when a person has a precognitive glimpse of the future, they are tuning into the future of that particular hologram only." According to Talbot, there are many holographic pictures "floating in the timeless and spaceless waters of the implicate (the enfolded order), jostling and swimming around one another like so many amoebas."

One of the basic tenets of quantum physics is that we are not merely discovering reality, but are partici-

---

* Michael Talbot, *The Holographic Universe*, HarperCollins, 1991.

pating in its creation. Dr. Loye says, "When we act upon a premonition and appear to alter the future, what we are really doing is leaping from one hologram to another." He calls these "*intra*holographic leaps" or "hololeaps" and feels that they are what provide us with our true capacity for both insight and freedom.

From my experience in the holographic heart, the future is indeed plastic and can be changed. I see it as composed of "crystallizing possibilities." Since everything is really interconnected, it's possible to tune in and choose a different holographic frequency pattern and change your future. You are very simply doing that when you follow your heart directives rather than your same old head program.

Your perspective at any given moment plays a significant part in creating the quality of your future. We are like artists, sculpting our destiny as we go. Most of us are unconscious participants in the patterns and frequencies of our holographic blueprint. But in becoming heart conscious, we activate new crystallizing possibilities that put us on the highest blueprint possible, God's plan for us. As it says in the Bible, "Eye hath not seen, nor ear heard, neither have entered into the heart of man, the things which God hath prepared for them that love him." (1 Corinthians 2:9)

In the holographic heart, I can see microchip records of antiquity, of All, and of the universe that goes beyond. The frequencies of the past and present unite to form a configuration of magnetics that draws a specific future holographic pattern into your present. Some of the strongest crystallizing possibilities of your holographic blueprint can be seen in major life events such as marriage, accidents, death and enlightenment experiences. Many people have had powerful glimpses of higher fourth and fifth dimensional awareness. Through their inner vision they have experienced the coming together of all forces of nature in blissful oneness. Or they have seen the pure pristine light within their core heart. Sincerely wanting to understand what you're here for, and wanting to do God's job for you better, puts you in apprenticeship to God.

Nature always seeks a balance, so the future patterns people magnetize are their system's effort to create balance. Disasters can teach us profound lessons that result in more understanding. Some people love and respect nature and learn balance from her harmony. As we learn to harmonize our lives, we help balance the holographic patterns in Mother Nature which humanity is part of. Perhaps then, Mother Nature wouldn't need to teach us to care for each other through storms and earthquakes. At least we can know she loves us enough to care that we learn one way or another. Each person still has choice. If you don't go to your heart and learn from a misfortune, you could magnetize similar frequencies to yourself (possibly another misfortune). When you use heart intelligence in life, you rearrange your future frequencies and often can avoid disasters.

From my experience, a fifth dimensional hololeap is possible when you view your filmstrip and then have the intelligence to erase or remodel part of your character. You can actually walk into the holographic heart and re-enact that part in the play. In other words, you give yourself a fresh start by going into your past and making a different choice. It's like taking out a particular computer chip, an old program, by altering the basic frequency. You come back to your everyday world, but with less baggage and a fresh perspective. Hololeaps could be considered a form of time travel.

One of my holographic experiences started while I was doing a Heart Lock-in one evening. I clearly saw a cartoon-like filmstrip. As I entered into it, everything took on a dreamlike quality. The next thing I remember is waking up. I didn't think much about it, got up and walked into another room. There I saw people and energy beings whom I didn't recognize. I also saw a transparent dome around the room. The tables and chairs were still there but had an ethereal look. I focused on one of the people and he slowly began to rotate. At each turn, the perspective and angle changed, revealing a different character. I felt connected to this person in the heart and realized I was seeing a multidimensional being. Another being who was both flowing and angular walked up then and sat down next to me. As he sat down, he folded up. It made me wonder in this moment if Lewis Carroll's *Alice in Wonderland* wasn't so far-fetched after all.

I wasn't sure if the usual objects in that room were real, so I took the cup in my hand and laid it down on the table. It was solid and I realized I was in two realities at the same time. A howling seemed to come from the trees outside and I went to look. Though I live on a ranch in the woods, I was surprised to see a wolf outside my door. I felt no fear as he walked towards me, then stopped. I saw the side of the transparent dome between myself and the wolf. He could go no further.

My heart intuition spoke in my thoughts, saying, "Holographic movies appear on the inside. A holodome appears outside around you, in your 3-D environment."

Afterwards I wondered — cartoons and people in the same movie? Then I remembered the movie *Roger Rabbit* in which people interact with cartoon characters. Perhaps imaginative artists like Walt Disney, who made cartoons popular, and Lewis Carroll were really tuning into holographic images!

Each moment is a doorway to time travel. Being in this very moment and no other, time as we know it stops. You Freeze-Frame and stop. Then you can make another choice. You can stay in the same holographic pattern or you can choose a different one. As I comprehended more universal principles concerning the hololeap, I occasionally peered into the future and saw the various crystallizing possibilities, realizing we truly do have a hand in their creation.

BEING IN THE MOMENT

Future events often cast a cloud's shadow in our present thoughts and in our daydreams of old memories. You might have a hunch that an old friend is going to call and thoughts wander into memories of old times together. And then the phone rings and it's that friend. I find the best way to prepare for future moments, or to stabilize any unwanted past moment, is to be fully in my present moment, *now*. To be in the now is a state of mind that doesn't stagnate in the past or the future. Living in the moment is living in the spirit — with buoyancy and sparkle — the spirit being the essence of life.

Practically speaking, let's say you're eating a hamburger on Tuesday while thinking of a steak dinner you're going to have next Friday. It's likely you are not enjoying the hamburger to its full potential. Being in the moment involves giving maximum appreciation and love to your present experience. This widens the doorway to the potential of the *Now*. As Doc Lew Childre states in his book *Self Empowerment,*

> "The Now Age is the age of individual (do-it-yourself) enlightenment—*Now!* Until this is implemented, stress will casually rule....I've experienced both new age and old age structures but decided it was more efficient to live in the 'now.' By the 'now,' I mean: *this moment.*"*

So how do you practically apply holography to the real world of this moment? When you see old patterns of fear arise, that's when you need to go to your heart intelligence for a wider perspective. Your next thoughts, feelings and actions will determine how the next hour and often the rest of your day unfolds. Your little choices really do count.

I vividly remember one such incident a few years ago. I saw a girlfriend of mine in an animated conversation with my boyfriend. They both seemed to be enjoying themselves and an old pattern of insecurity arose inside me. My stomach clenched. "Maybe he likes her more than me," I thought. Jealousy and fear started to color my perceptions. My head ran automatic thoughts of, "I'm not as pretty as she is," "I don't communicate as well as she does," "he might spend less time with me," "he might even leave me." I stopped it right there. I knew from experience exactly where that train of thought would lead. Right into a wall! Right into me cutting off my heart to protect myself from rejection.

---

*Available from Planetary Publications. See page 272.

When I'd done this before, my boyfriend, sensing my coldness, would withdraw from me. Inevitably, an argument and a miserable day would follow. By consciously choosing to Freeze-Frame, go back to the heart, and sincerely love them both, my perspective totally changed. I could see they were innocently enjoying conversation with each other. It was no big deal. I realized they both loved me. In stopping fearful thoughts, I leaped to another "holodome," and actually changed my future. The rest of my day was wonderful!

Holograms are really like a hall of mirrors. It's whatever perspective you want to see, whatever angle you look at in the mirror, that determines your reality. Stopping head thoughts to gain a wider perspective of the moment *is* the choice of creation. Only through the heart can one see the holographic movie objectively. When your heart directs you to leap into another holodome, do it and surrender to the new movie. Participate in it and experience it fully. That activates your next heart-directed program, and the next, and you move on in your highest blueprint in the universal flow.

Intraholographic leaps on the vertical or horizontal axis of the energy grid of life can be viewed as an inter-dimensional chess game between you and you. The vertical axis is moving inward into higher understandings of yourself and life. The horizontal axis is widening your love of people and experiencing them at deeper levels of understanding. At times your heart directs you to go within for more awareness. At other times it directs you to radiate your love outward and connect more with life. Evolution is about balancing these two axes to activate the higher holographic frequencies and enter into the higher dimensions.

The holographic movie of daily life can seem so solid and real — from the moment you wake up to the moment you go to sleep. After all, each day you live in the same house, in the same city, with the same sun shining through your window, and the same trees outside your door. Your mind/brain/body gets used to this, so reality appears very solid and third dimensional. As I was going to sleep one night, I experienced all three dimensions, third, fourth and fifth, as distinct realities. Each was as real as the 3-D world we live in. I saw moving through dimensions as the vertical axis. Then I saw the head and heart choices we make in life as the horizontal axis. When you dream at night, have you ever considered whether your consciousness is in another dimensional reality? Or, have you considered whether, right now, you are somewhere sleeping and this waking life is your dream? Could you have parallel realities, or parallel worlds, going on?

Different holographic filmstrips could be viewed as parallel worlds. Our personal filmstrips often have us acting out the same basic frequency but with different "furniture." It's like living several movies with essentially the same plot, but with different actors, different sets, and the potential for different outcomes. How many times do people tell themselves, "I've been through this *so* many times before." Many people marry, divorce and marry again, only to find the same movie playing out again in the new marriage. In dreams at night, we often act out the same frequency patterns we experienced in the day, but with different characters and scenes.

In his best selling novel, *One*, Richard Bach used a combination of personal experience and fiction to describe his understanding of what it's like moving in and out of parallel realities. While much of what I am writing here is rather abstract, I hope my words and experience can give you at least a feeling for the timeless, overlapping qualities and potential of the holographic heart.

God created the sun, the water, the stars, the natural environment, people, the universe. They are all universal holographic creations, made real by our heart/mind/brain perceptions. As we become holographically aware, we can enter into them, just as we can a holographic 3-D picture today. *Appreciation and love in the moment are the key.* Appreciate and love the sun, the water, whatever you are gazing on. Appreciation magnetizes their holographic images and patterns to you, so you can dance and co-create with their essence. In this way the whole universal hologram expands, evolves and grows. This oneness is the next step in human evolution. Co-creation is where evolution and creation are understood as one.

Each of us is responsible for our spectrum of perspectives in the holographic creation because we really do have choice. "Do the starving people in Africa have choice?" you may ask. They don't have the immediate choice to eat if there's no food, but they do have choice to stay in the heart or not. By staying in the heart, they might possibly magnetize more heart from those who have the food to give them. Being angry and resentful won't bring food any faster, and it only makes you more miserable. Have compassion and understanding for those enduring hardship. Every human has their own holographic blueprint, with its own crystallizing possibilities. But this doesn't mean we ignore their suffering. In the heart we would sincerely want to help.

In the movie you are living *today*, are you choosing a heart perspective or a head perspective? Depending on your choice, you will write different sequences for your day and the consequences will be different — activating different holographic filmstrips. The highest intelligence has "streetsense" in the choices it makes, streetsense being the common sense of the heart which integrates and aligns higher fourth dimensional perceptions into the 3-D world here and now. Streetsense contains complexity broken down into simple understandings. It's a practical, balanced, and efficient approach to a life situation that simply "makes sense." Streetsense is the road to clear perception about what *is*.

THE PART AND THE WHOLE

"To see a World in a Grain of Sand

And a Heaven in a Wild Flower

Hold Infinity in the palm of your hand

And Eternity in an hour."

   William Blake

The basic holographic principle is that every part contains the whole. In holography, every piece of a holographic picture contains the entire picture. In the now famous experiment called, "The Phantom Leaf Effect," an electrophotograph of an amputated leaf revealed a picture of an intact, whole leaf. The amputated portion still appeared in the photo of the leaf, even though the missing leaf fragment had been destroyed. In another scientific experiment conducted in Rumania, Dr. I. Dumitrescu cut a circular hole in a leaf, then recorded it by electrophotography. The photographic image revealed a small leaf with a hole in it, which appeared inside the hole where the leaf had been cut. Inside the hole in the small leaf appeared another smaller leaf with a hole in it.

How is it possible to take a picture of something not physically there? The piece that was cut out left the information of the whole electrically recorded in a nonphysical field! But, this information also contained a leaf appearing inside a leaf and another leaf inside that leaf, like a mirror effect, confirming the holographic nature of the organizing energy field (etheric grid or etheric body) that surrounds all living organisms. This etheric grid is in reality a holographic energy pattern. The entire universe can be seen as one large, dynamically changing, energy pattern.

Every tiny cell in your body contains an identical copy of your master DNA blueprint. As Richard Gerber, M.D., author of *Vibrational Medicine*, states,

> "The fact that every cell within the human body contains the exact same information to create an entire duplicate body mirrors the holographic principle whereby every piece contains the information of the whole."*

Like the phantom leaf, your master DNA blueprint is holographically mirrored in every cell of your body. When you hold a tiny acorn in your hand, you know it contains the entire blueprint for a huge oak tree. You also know that when a sperm and ovum come together, they contain the entire blueprint for an adult human.

---

* Richard Gerber, M.D., *Vibrational Medicine*, (Bear & Co., 1988)

Imagine every cell in your body also containing the frequency blueprint of the whole universe. Only through the heart can you access these higher dimensional perceptions of universal frequency structures. The bioenergetic field of the physical body is a holographic energy template with encoded information of All. It contains the DNA blueprint of the fetus along with a road map for cellular repair in the event of damage to the developing organism. The medical question arises, "Is it possible to enter into and communicate with the DNA holographic blueprint pattern to improve health and cure diseases?"

FUTURE SCIENCE

Researcher Daniel Winter, in conjunction with the Institute of HeartMath, has been mapping the electrical and sonic links between cardiac electricities, mental processes, emotions, and brain electricities. Winter is especially interested in the relationship between DNA programming and immune health.

Winter and the Institute used spectrum analysis of EKG tests on subjects who were practiced in sending out conscious love. They made significant discoveries. Winter states,

> "When love was being sent to someone, the spectrum analysis of the EKG revealed a ratio between the frequency peaks of 1.618, the *Golden Mean*. The ratio of the Golden Mean, 1.618, is the most efficient ratio known for the transfer of energy between scales. When energy is phase locked with this ratio it cascades between octaves without losing momentum or memory of itself. The fractal design of the heart uses this principle to send energy cascading down the harmonic series to the DNA.

The geometry of these waves looks exactly like the DNA as viewed from the top. The main point here is that 1.618 is also the ratio of the DNA structure and is the only ratio that allows complete information or geometry to cascade down the harmonic series without loss of power or geometry. Loving causes the coherence and ratio necessary to send energy up or down the harmonic series from the higher organizational dimensions down to the DNA. In a sense, no directions radiate to the DNA and immune system from the heart, unless there is a conscious link-up to the core of one's being. By loving and caring it is possible to reprogram and empower the DNA with the intelligence of working for the whole from the perspective of higher electrical energy dimensions."

The implications of this research are profound. By sending coherent heart frequencies of conscious love and care, people can enter into the DNA, and reprogram and empower it to improve immune system and cellular health. Universal love embraces, protects, nurtures and communicates to the DNA to unfold its blueprint. This communication cascades on frequency harmonics of the golden mean spiral. Only through sincere love and care from the core of being in the heart, can we enter into God's design and co-create at the holographic level of the DNA. The heart is the protective safety valve. This is very different from genetic engineering as we know it now, which is only tinkering with the components of the gene on the physical level.

COMING HOME

Within your DNA is the golden means back to your origin, your primary source or cause; therein lies the frequency path to "Home." This particular DNA doorway is contained in the hidden power of the heart. As your awakening process unfolds, the DNA codes are unveiled to your awareness, creating the understanding of the power and potential of primal "Love." Love the saints and sages of this world who understood that each cell in your system contained the creation of the whole universe. They expressed their knowledge in language understandable to their times. Now, with new scientific language, the third dimensional mind can understand the unveiling of the mysteries of life. St. Thomas Aquinas said, "Since God is the universal cause of all Being, in whatever region Being can be found, there must be the Divine Presence." This is the concept of hologramatic biology. It is a biology that would allow God, your Creator, to clothe part of His eternal awareness in material form.

God consciousness utilized a delicate synthesis of two methods of creation, one deliberate and the other allowing. For people to co-create in the universal order, there had to be allowing — free choice. Jesus was referring to this co-creative process when he said, "Ye are all gods." And, "Verily, verily, I say unto you, He that believeth on me, the works that I do shall he do also; and greater works than these shall he do; because I go unto my Father." The human DNA is a deliberate primal self-replicating particle/entity of God, created in an environment conducive to the kind of development the Creator wanted to see — God's plan. Then, the *hope* was that the DNA creation would freely choose of its own will to pursue development in the frequency of love, the frequency of its Creator. The Creator's plan can be seen in the innate desire of parents to see their children have loving and fulfilled lives. When a child is unloving or hurtful to others, the parent disciplines him, not to hurt him, but to help him become more loving .

How can humanity activate God's plan in the DNA? Consider what would happen if everyone in the world decided to love the best they knew how, for just ten minutes at the same time on the same day. There have been efforts to synchronize masses of people in prayer or meditation at the same time. Harmonic Convergence and Hands Across America were two such efforts. What if we asked people to just try to be in the heart and love for ten minutes? Millions of people focusing simply on love would set off a new holographic frequency — generating a quantum leap. It would be like jump starting a battery; once it's charged it can empower the whole.

The Divine Purpose embedded in the DNA template is to bring all humans into hologramatic consciousness, understanding the universe with the same attunement that Christ had. However, you must not merely attune to the rhythms and frequencies of the whole but also participate in them freely, through your own will. Imagine how happy the Creator would be if everyone, at the same point in time, would choose to love! It would signal a new holographic program, triggering the fulfillment of the Divine Purpose.

Humanity will soon awaken to the realization that evolutionary unfoldment has a geometric progression, the Golden Mean ratio, that is characteristic of harmonic radiations of love. As Dan Winter states, "Clearly there is some elegant function accomplished by the weaving of all this essence of geometry into gene stuff." It unfolds the Creator's intention.

The Golden Mean ratio is a perfect bridge for bringing waves of different lengths into coherence. The Golden Mean ratio harmonizes waves through balance. "Coherence" in this context is used to define two or more wave forms that are "phase-locked" together (locked in phase with each other) so their energy is constructive. In other words, the Golden Mean acts a bridge that organizes your frequencies to work together without friction. Your DNA structure is designed *so the choice to function in love is the only choice that brings you fulfillment.* Stress is inner biofeedback, signaling you that frequencies are fighting within your system. The purpose of stress isn't to hurt you, but to let you know it's time to go back to the heart and start loving.

The joint research project with Dan Winter and the Institute of HeartMath also showed that heart electricities contain an encoded intelligence. They concluded that the heart acts as a transformer for intelligence which allows a two-way communication between different dimensions. The heart is the doorway to the highly organized intelligence that programs the DNA. Intui-Technology™ is the aspect of the HeartMath system that walks you through any holographic program so you can access the Golden Mean frequency any moment of the day. With practice, Intui-Technology leads you from third dimensional awareness to fourth and fifth dimensional heart intelligence. Freeze-Frame is one of the key tools to unfold this heart intelligence.

The term coherence also describes a single wave form that has an ordered distribution of its power content. Going from incoherent, random mental and emotional energy expenditures to coherent energy is powerful. It's like the difference between incandescent light (which is random and incoherent) and the brilliant energy of a laser beam (which is focused and coherent). The key principle is that coherent consciousness can go beyond ordinary waking consciousness.

The research also revealed that *heart electricities are shown to be coherent when an individual is highly focused on loving or appreciating someone or something.* It is well known by doctors and reseachers that heart electricity is the dominant force in the human system. When the heart is radiating coherent energy patterns, it causes the electricities of the brain and its sub-centers (the head) to phase-lock with the heart patterns, creating greater efficiency. This research has shown a direct correlation between the frequency signature of cardiac electricity and positive mental and emotional states. The geometric ratios, as seen in the rhythm, amplitude and frequency modulation of heart electricities, also appear harmonically linked to the physical cellular system, the immune system and DNA structure.

Heart intelligence is essentially able to download a broader frequency bandwidth of harmonic instruction when the heart fires (or beats) in a relaxed but centered state of "phase-locked" resonance. Coherent (focused) love permits a greater content of these harmonic instructions from the heart to be downloaded from the longer waves of the higher dimensions into the shorter waves of the DNA, from etheric energy to matter. The shape which illustrates this process is the Golden Mean spiral. This Golden Mean pathway also permits the process to function in reverse — from matter to energy, from short wave to long. The communication goes two ways at once. The geometric Golden Mean spiral shape actually looks like the fractal* image of the heart itself.

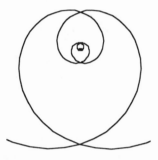

The principle of energy interference among waves of any type (sound, light, water, etc.) is that order (or constructive interference) self-replicates, while disorder (or destructive interference) self-destructs. Simply put, this means you can boost a wave's amplitude by attuning to its frequency, or you can disrupt a wave by introducing a dissonant frequency. Heart perspective brings waves into focus. The points of resonant convergence are where lines of energy and intention meet. The results of the joint research project showed that coherent emotional waves, like love, are self-regenerating, teachable, and easily accessible with practice.

Through love and attunement with your "spirit," you resonate with the field of universal spirit, God. Through your conscious human eyes, you will be able to see and understand things as the universe itself does. This perspective works both ways. Universal intelli-

---

* Fractal objects are objects that are composed of sub-units that resemble the larger scale shape. These sub-units are in turn composed of yet smaller sub-units that also look similar to the larger one and so on. (Like the repeating fractal image in the Phantom Leaf electrophotograph.) Mathematically speaking, fractals maintain the same ratio while changing scale. The Golden Mean spiral is the geometric template of the heart, which is its fractal counterpart in density.

gence can also look through the human soul, to see into the very depths of the world of matter. You can consciously participate in the Golden Mean two-way communication cascade between the higher dimensions and the DNA. You see into the patterns of cosmic structure, in the macrocosm and in the microcosm, using your heart intelligence, decoding your DNA, enabling you to see what *is*, and what is to come.

In holographic creation, it's not prophecy that gives you this kind of future vision. Nor does this vision stem from some latent, undiscovered part of the human mind. Vision enables you to glimpse into the future, to sense its hope and its power, because you yourself are the means of that future's creation. You are part of the hologram that is!

INCREASING THE LIGHT

As more higher dimensional energy comes into the planet, more vision will be possible. There will be tremendous scientific and technological breakthroughs throughout the next twenty years. This period of high technological emphasis will serve the whole world. It will serve the purpose of creative intelligence in ways yet undreamed of. Science will no longer deny the spirit within, but will assist in the material implementation of the spirit's implicit designs and patterns. Fueled by divine motivation, technology will take leaps that will make the twentieth century look like the dark ages.

You can see intelligence in all life forms. You can also see it in our own species, in our sperm, ova, chromosomes — our DNA holographic template. At the Institute, through our research to unfold the principles of holographic medicine, we are embarking on test projects with AIDS patients. Associates at the Institute would send focused love — coherent heart energy — while AIDS patients practice the tools of the HeartMath system, attuning to their own heart frequencies. Immune system tests, such as T-cell counts, would be used to determine if there is improvement in cell health. Psychological testing would follow to see whether stress levels were reduced and well-being enhanced.

As more pilot studies unravel "holographic medicine," the possibilities become limitless. There will be an accepted medical understanding that what happens in just a small fragment of the holographic energy pattern affects the entire structure simultaneously. There is a tremendous connectedness between all parts of the holographic universe.

I'm not a physicist or a mathematician, yet I intuitively understand all this abstract physics and geometry. An answer to mitigating or curing AIDS, cancer and other diseases would be found in their holographic characteristics. Every piece of the universe not only "contains," but also holographically "contributes" to the information of the whole. To enter into one cell holographically changes all the cells. How else would Christ cure the blind, the deaf, and the crippled from birth? Christ healed with higher fourth dimensional awareness, and it was a miracle to most people. His disciples healed also by accessing those frequencies.

With the fifth dimensional energies coming into the planetary energy grid, people will be able to see more of the whole picture. They will see how to totally dissipate the cross-frequencies in their systems — physical, emotional, mental, spiritual. That's what holistic health is really about — healing your own self.

Holographic medicine will bring *holographic health* into being. People with holographic awareness will be able, with permission, to enter the subconscious and unconscious holographic filmstrips of a sick person and change the frequency patterns that caused the illness. That person would have to be responsible for sustaining the new perspective this would give them. Christ often said to those he healed, "Go your way and sin no more," meaning stay in the new perspective you now have. By learning to follow your heart, you will sustain the new perspective.

Holographic breakthroughs will lead us to a totally new understanding of what reality is. Michael Talbot sums it up,

> "The objective world does not exist, at least not in the way we are accustomed to believing. What is 'out there' is a vast ocean of waves and frequencies and reality looks concrete to us only because our brains are able to take this holographic blur and convert it into sticks and stones and other familiar objects that make up our world."

As people's consciousness transitions from the third dimensional perspective to the higher fourth, humanity will wake up to what really *is*.

During the next twenty years, through the simple practice of living from the heart, those who have understood enough of what the "love" frequency is about will, themselves, be able to sustain the higher dimensional frequencies for others as the creation veil is lifted. This will enable more people to make a clear, conscious choice to love or not.

The hidden power of the heart would not be so magnificent and powerful if it weren't this simple. Whether you are an illiterate migrant worker, a high school drop-out, or a have a college degree, you will experience the lifting of the creation veil if you choose to love. Those who do not make the choice to consciously love will find themselves in another holographic reality where they can learn to love — not on this planet. By approximately the year 2011, the human race will have reached its due date for this transition. Mother Earth and all people who share her holographic field in consciousness will be prepared for this birth into the higher fourth dimension. No one knows for sure if the united birth of humanity into this new awareness will be before the due date or later.

This transition will be as great as the first cellular assemblies some 3.5 billion years ago. It is a significant leap in the unfoldment of universal order. The development of the planet, from God to the first DNA particle/entity of God that evolved from amoeba to human over billions of years, was a process incorporating hololeaps in biological order, not unlike the incarnation of the soul and the development of the fetus from a single sperm and ovum. The completion of this particular human cycle of evolution will be realized as humanity moves into holographic God conscious awareness. Don't just take my word for it. Practice conscious loving and living in the heart of each moment and let the truth unfold from within you.

Chapter 16

DNA Blueprints

Y our holographic heart crystals imprint their electrical patterns and programs in your DNA. As you activate new heart programs, they are communicated directly to your DNA. Like the heart crystals, the DNA structure has the core frequency of "love" as its bottom line frequency grid. The human body is a composite of intricate and interwoven frequencies that are biological patterns imprinted in the DNA. The DNA takes responsibility for creation. Historically, for the first time, as we move into the higher dimensional awareness, the entire human family will emerge into a totally new cycle of creation. As your vibrational frequencies awaken, you will understand your human circuitry for what it is. You must use your highest intelligence as your guide. This type of energy management leads to making consistently efficient decisions that are fulfilling. They keep you on your highest blueprint.

In day-to-day life, inefficient choices aren't wrong since there is no wrong in evolution. They just take you around the block on a longer journey than necessary to reach your destination and fulfill your DNA blueprint. It takes even longer if you add self-judgment, overcare, or guilt. We've all done this, so it's no big deal — it's just not efficient and not very fun.

The best way to understand your blueprint is to imagine a city map. You have to navigate the city with all its one-way streets, left and right-hand turns, traffic jams, and detours. In this city, each time you take a left-hand turn it drains your energy because it's not the most efficient way to get you where you want to go. So when you turn left, you get stress feedback in your feeling world in the form of tension, anxiety, repression, and guilt. This is not to punish you; it has a purpose. It's a signal to help you change your course to get back on the right track — in the universal flow. Traffic jams are like hesitations along the way. You get into a bottle-neck because you aren't practicing what you know you should be doing. Detours are like side trips, life geometries that bring you expansion in often unexpected areas to help you learn and grow.

When you make a "left-hand turn" in life, your heart computer will try to help you get back on track. It will try to help you make a right-hand turn, then another right, and another right, to get you back around the block to where you were going in the first place. Left-hand turns can happen in the smallest situations of life or the biggest. One small example of a left-hand turn in my life was when I wanted to borrow a recipe from a friend for a party I was planning later in the week.

I had a feeling to call her on the phone first, but I didn't. I went over to her house and arrived when she was in the middle of entertaining guests. She was obviously uncomfortable and told me to call her later that day. But I was so embarrassed that I didn't. It was two days before I had the courage to call her. She wasn't home and we kept playing telephone tag. I spent hours frantically searching for another recipe for the main course. Finally, she returned my call just as I was about to go shopping for the party. The dinner turned out fine, but what a waste of time and energy just because I didn't listen to my common sense feelings that told me to call her first. Left-hand turns take longer and are just more work for yourself. Right-hand turns are the product of listening to and following your heart computer, living life through the spirit.

Your little, everyday choices really do count in the unfoldment of your blueprint. If you're not sure which way to go in making decisions, stay in the heart and love, radiate heart energy until your heart computer kicks in with a read-out. You will increasingly make choices that activate your higher frequencies. That's creating heaven on earth for yourself through "care." It means taking the time to go to your higher intelligence for direction. With practice, it doesn't take much time, and direction comes as quick, spontaneous intuition.

The most efficient way to understand the universal principles is to understand your own self in day-to-day life. The puzzle pieces or events in a day are your life geometries for experiencing and expanding awareness. Making right-hand turns and following your highest blueprint will lead you to your mission in life and activate your passion to be all you can be. It builds real self-esteem that lasts. Those who make continual efforts to self-manage their energies from the heart over the next ten years will have increased fun and fulfillment in life. Those who continue to operate mostly from head bands, will experience increased stress — head processors feeding back on themselves.

The next decade will accelerate the polarization of people's choices, either to go back to the heart to bail out, or remain imprisoned in the stress they are creating. The incoming frequencies are loving, but neutral. It is you who qualifies what the energy does inside you by operating from the heart or the head. You accumulate assets or deficits in your energy system relative to the peace or the stress you have. As you observe your overall level of peace, you can determine the real quality of your life. It's simple math.

Love is the energy of expansion, the vital current of creation. The thoughts you create generate the patterns that shape your environment. With planetary acceleration of energies, people's stressful thoughts will create patterns so they either break down on some level (the inner Armageddon) or wake up and realize they have to go back to the heart. The energies of light and love coming into the planet are a universal effort to help humanity. They form a mathematical equation of eternity — union with the heaven worlds, union with your own Christ self, and union with the people. You do your 1, step-by-step, and you get a 9 in energy return. Historically, this hasn't always been the case. It used to feel like the best you could do was to take three steps forward and two back. But in the new ratio of intelligence entering the planetary system today, you receive back more light and love than you put out — in a ratio of 9:1. It's like extremely high interest on your bank account — your energy management account. This is the power of the higher dimensional energy equation accelerating the planet.

Light is something that makes vision possible. Love makes feeling possible. As I practice loving more sincerely, I increasingly see and feel more light in my human energy field. I am able to watch the unfoldment of my energy system and feel changes in its patterns. The human energy field absorbs light and reradiates it through a system of spiraling energy centers along the spine and brain. I can see the bottom sexual center, the solar plexus, the crown center, and other centers. These centers have varying degrees of amp and power. Together, they form the actual physical substance of the light fixture of my system. The light bulb by which I can see and experience this light fixture is formed by the holographic crystals in my heart.

This realization stimulated yet another illumination — a series of light bulbs going off in my head, forming intelligent thoughts, colors, patterns and codes. Focusing on these patterns and codes, I began to read my DNA blueprint and saw how my practice of living in the heart had put me on my highest blueprint. I saw in the DNA structure of my human body a holographic pattern of the entire universe in miniature. I was entering deeper into the mystery of creation and evolution. I was part of the process even as I was viewing it.

I realized that the Big Bang resulted from the core heart frequency of love. It was the pure essence of Love itself. Love couldn't contain its own love and had to expand. It created heat and light, bursting forth like an orgasm. Love created male and female to explore, expand and create more love.

As Jesus said,

"Ye are the light of the world. A city that is set on a hill cannot be hid. Neither do men light a candle and put it under a bushel, but on a candlestick, and it gives light to all that are in the house." (Matthew 5:14)

Heart power creates illumination. If you forget your heart crystals (your light bulb), you will have power in darkness. So you can't forget your heart. The quickest way to illuminate the entire planet is to plug your own system into your heart, then love the people, and use that love as current for the light. It creates a giant electrical circuit of light coming through you to others, and helps light go through them also. Everyone has free will and choice and can choose to receive that light or not. It's still up to you and yourself. It's your perspective.

Chapter 17

Return to Family Values

C reation is the evolution of the Family Tree. In common-sense terms, we know that male and female
together create the child, a process that evolves the family tree. The Bible contains page after page of who be-
got who. Ancestry is important to all native cultures,
and family genealogy is popular with many people in
the '90s as they search their heritage for identity and
roots. My own father has diligently traced my mother's
side of our family tree back to the 1500s.

Discovering our divine heritage in the DNA brings
a deeper understanding of the real purpose of family.
In the Bible, Jesus states: "The first and great commandment [frequencies of Universal Laws] is, 'Thou shalt love
the Lord thy God [love your Creator] with all thy heart,
and with all thy soul, and with all thy mind.' And the
second is like unto it: 'Thou shalt love thy neighbor as
thyself.' On these two commandments hang all the law

and the prophets." (Matthew 23: 37-40) This often quoted Bible verse is deeply encoded with higher intelligence.

Loving your neighbor doesn't just mean the person who lives next door or on the same block. Planet Earth is but one big yard — the evolution of one family tree from the original DNA. We're all neighbors and we're all part of the family of Mother Earth. You would want to love your neighbor if only to gain an understanding of your total self.

Practicing the heart power tool of "loving the people" facilitated a tremendous expansion in my awareness. It's my tool of choice. If I ever want more understanding about anything — whether a predicament in my life, direct perception of another person, or about some aspect of the universe — I start by loving the people. I understood Jesus' true meaning when he said, "A new commandment I give unto you, That ye love one another; as I have loved you, that ye also love another." Loving the people is what gives you the power to turn on the computer chips in the heart crystals that contain the information you want.

I start by using my head to clearly formulate a question. Then I focus my mind and all my energies deep in my heart, and start loving people. That activates the sincere core heart frequency of love. Connecting with your own deeper heart, and then with other people's hearts, creates a tremendous power circuit. It creates the access code to the mysteries of the universe. The answers don't necessarily come in the way you might expect. They come as your next step in unfoldment, the next frequency of your blueprint that you need in order to understand the next, and so on.

Allow love free access to your heart and mind. There, the deepest intelligence between Creator and creation is designed and destined to occur. The heart motive of any effective religious or self-help system is to facilitate people to get in touch with the teacher, church, master, and Creator within their own system. You build your foundation, or frequency board, to hold more current by using your heart computer to translate all the data from your mind, feelings or senses.

When you're in love fully, without reservation, you feel and move with the universal rhythmic current: Love. In the awakened state, the higher fourth and fifth dimensional awareness, you not only perceive the physical world, but also the spirit world, the world of hope and potential in God's cosmic design.

DISCOVERING THE FAMILY FREQUENCY

As I practiced loving the people in all situations, or at least made the effort to try, I came in touch with the essence of the "Family Frequency." This frequency is the deeper, personal love and care for every person, plant or animal on the planet. The Family Frequency embraces the earth as all one family, a global or planetary family. This frequency comes from the higher dimensions as a truly new *understanding*. It's the realization that everyone really is connected to each other in the heart. It's an experience of oneness with Mother Earth herself. The family frequency band unfolds as people align themselves in the heart, communicating, working, and living as *all for one and one for all*. It's a powerful band of energy that helps you realize, understand, feel, and experience the *eternal* security of oneness.

A family of holographically aware beings of love and light is sending a powerful family frequency to earth. It's a frequency that cares about you. The revival of interest in family values is the result of this infusion of care. Sincere family feelings come from the heart. They bring hope for real security and peace in this stressful world. The compassion of beings who know the eternal nature, while living on Earth, *can* bring the world to peace. Eternal awareness would know the divine intentions of the Creator. By living in a human body and practicing being in the heart, holographically aware beings could show the human family how to access the universal plan. As Christ said of himself and his disciples, "They are not of this world, even as I am not of this world." (John 17:16) He had taught them how to be in the world, yet be guided by their spirit rather than locked into the frequency perspectives of the second and third dimensions.

Humanity is regaining an appreciation for "family" and will continue to do so. In a support group of family, people look out for each other and accept people for who they are. A family grows and moves through life together, inseparable in the heart. A family acts as a buffer to external distortions. A family made up of self-secure people generates a magnetic power that can get things done. As people live in this family frequency, they animate other people's heart bands, making it easier for them to wake up and experience the love and security needed to understand *all that is*.

Real family values don't demand a return to old family structures. There are thousands of traditional, nuclear families who are family in name only. Real family is a deep feeling inside, the recognition of an inner need for support and security. Family would include the extended family, people attracted to each other based on heart resonance and mutual support.

As we move into the next millennium (the next 10-20 years), there will be a serious awakening to the family frequency. This will bring tremendous hope to the world. It will awaken within one's heart and spirit the same motivation to care or love, that a mother or father feels toward their child. When people fall in love with "love" itself, the new world has begun. It is a new world of perception, a new world of understanding, a world where resources are only limited by the capacity to appreciate.

THE INNER FAMILY

All aspects of yourself can be found in your heart, including your "inner family." Your inner family is your inner "mom," your inner "dad," and your inner "child." Your higher self is a family of these three aspects. The balancing of male, female, and childlike frequencies is the cornerstone of self-empowerment. You can learn to combine these three aspects in yourself — the nurturing, the self-activating, and the childlike spontaneity. It's important to distinguish between childish and childlike. The true inner child is your *childlike* spirit, not the whiny, complaining child.

One day, I decided to ask my inner family how to approach one of the engineers at the Institute, John. He has an aggressive personality and often intimidated others. I asked my inner "dad" for perspective. I felt a strong male frequency within my heart. My intuition showed me how this co-worker really got a lot done, that he was a dynamic self-starter who really tried to cut through obstacles. I could appreciate those qualities in him. Then I asked my inner "mom" for a perspective. I felt a softer frequency come into my heart. My intuition showed me that this man had a very sensitive side with which he wasn't always comfortable. The mom in me suggested I have more heart, compassion and understanding for him, and talk to his sensitive side — that would help him gain more balance and security within himself. I really enjoyed this dialogue with my inner family. The frequencies felt wonderful and the wisdom made sense. When I tuned into my inner child and asked for a childlike perspective, I was able to see the child in this man, and how he delighted in jumping into any new project. I could also see that as he learned to balance his aggressive love of action with his more sensitive side, his inner child would be much happier and feel freer to express. He would no longer intimidate others. I intuited that if I, too, were a little more spontaneous and childlike with him, it would help our communications. All together, these three aspects of myself gave me a wide and fairly complete picture of the situation. The best part of the story is this: the next time we talked I remembered to do what my inner family had directed, and we had the deepest communication ever. My inner family was helping me to become my whole self.

Many adults today are involved in self-help practices to reconnect with their inner child and resolve old issues with their mother or father. This process can be accelerated by realizing you have your own inner family as a resource. You can experience the most positive, creative essence of the dad, mom and child within yourself.

From a heart understanding, your inner family is all one. Your outer family is the world — one big family in one big back yard — and the universe is one large city. Discover your Creator by learning to see any person on the planet as part of one big family. Maybe they are your 5,559th cousin. People have made divisions with the mind, but from an embracing global perspective, from a heart understanding, we are all one.

FAMILY VALUES

Many believe our modern world is out of balance because of a decline in family values. There are tremendous male/female/family issues absorbing the attention of our society. Most people feel that children today are not learning the *basic core values* of life. These are values that people believe are essential, involving a sense of personal and social responsibility. But if we want our children to be more efficient and mature with their energies, then we need to reach a new level of efficiency within ourselves. We can only give what we have.

Most people consider values like honesty, integrity and respect for others to be basic family values that parents should impart. But parents say they are frustrated by a lack of time to supervise their children and most feel guilty about it.

Surveys show that more parents than ever are giving themselves poor marks on child-rearing. As a result many parents feel their kids are undisciplined and lack morals. My sister Sallie worked in a school and found that each year there were more discipline problems, more fights, and more disturbed children. From my experience as a single working mother, the answer is putting a higher quality of attention into the few minutes Christian and I have together so the time's not wasted. We have the best heart contacts in no time at all. Einstein showed us time is an illusion. When you increase the quality of the input, the quality of the output has to increase. In a 1991 LOS ANGELES TIMES poll of Orange County residents, 53% of parents gave themselves a C grade in teaching their children morals, 25% of parents gave themselves a D or an F. This means that one-fourth of these largely middle to upper-middle class Americans feel they are about to fail, or are failing, in teaching their children "core values." What values are children learning and from where? From television? Movies? From the streets?

Which core values are we as a society neglecting the most? A series of surveys by the Massachusetts Mutual Life Insurance Company found that 70% or more of all Americans believe that the most important family values are: 1) being responsible for one's actions, 2) respecting other people for who they are, and 3) providing emotional support for one's family. In summary, Americans say that core family values represent responsibility, respect, and love.

Much has been written about how the structure of today's family differs from what it was in the past. In the '50s, the nuclear family consisted of a mother, a father and children. Today, there are more single parent families, families in which the parents are not married or are of the same sex, and households with children from different marriages. Some children have two or three step-mothers or step-fathers before they reach adulthood. Statistics reveal that each year, over 1,000,000 children in the USA are affected by divorce. Of these children, 50% grow up in families where their parents stay angry and 60% feel rejected by at least one parent. According to research compiled by Zinsmeister, more than 80% of adolescents in psychiatric hospitals come from broken families. Approximately three out of four teenage suicides occur in households where a parent has been absent. In our country, 33% of all children never see one of their parents again after they divorce.

Is it any wonder that today's children are increasingly involved in violent crimes, drug abuse and burglary? Juvenile delinquency statistics and drug use are climbing at a horrendous rate. Studies show that children have a harder time saying no to drugs when they lack family bonding. Many kids who take drugs say they don't feel loved, while many parents don't know how to help their children feel loved, accepted and appreciated. However, the closer children feel to their parents, the better equipped they are to resist self-destructive behavior.

It's hard for kids to "just say no" to drugs, due to frustration, loneliness, hopelessness and fear. A study at California's Marin County Community Mental Health Center revealed that in most divorces, children feel guilt, a loss of love, self-esteem and confidence. They believe they're to blame for the divorce, especially if it was bitter. Children who lose contact with a parent after divorce have pronounced instances of emotional disturbances. Parents can get so involved in hating each other as they separate and divorce, they often tell a child the other parent is no good and create hate in the child.

What's the main cause of divorce? Divorce results when one partner (or both) doesn't *feel loved* or *respected* by the other. When people feel this way, they find things to fight and argue about. If they don't fight, they just bury their emotions inside and create a wall. Soon there is no juice or connection and they start to feel numb. No wonder children of divorced parents have a hard time. They are coming from an environment where their parents didn't have the basic core values — love and respect — for each other. Unless society changes, do the kids of the '90s even have a chance? When they become adults, won't it be far more difficult for them to sustain a sense of community and build basic core values?

Whether you were raised in a traditional nuclear family structure, or are living in one of the new family structures of the '90s, the key to family bonding and unity is found in the core heart value of love. Love your children, respect them, and teach them respect for others. I am now a divorced parent and face the challenge of raising my ten year-old without his father living with us. I always go back to the core values of my heart for guidance. His father and I have a better friendship now than when we were married. He lives close by and sees Christian once a week, so there is a feeling of an extended family. The heart has been our bailout in making the divorce harmonious.

There is a great deal of concern in society about the increasing number of teenage gangs, not just in the inner cities but in suburbs, in small towns, on military bases — everywhere. When I was in high school, there were cliques of young people with different interests but not what I'd call gangs. Don't gangs offer children a substitute family structure? Gangs operate by their own core values and "codes of honor." In many instances, gang members are responsible for, respect, and love each other. They provide teenagers with an experience of family bonding, even though their gang activities are often violent and destructive. One positive outcome of the recent Los Angeles riots is that segments of the two most infamous gangs, the Bloods and the Cripps, decided to come together and stop killing each other. Somehow, they recognized "family" in each other. Gang behavior can be turned around as gangs learn to expand their family feeling through love and care for everyone.

If children were taught how to be responsible for themselves, then they would have the ability to serve and become responsible for others, their environment, their society, their world. The heart is our only hope for rebuilding common values in our stressed-out world. As people experience heart resonance through understanding and care, real "family values" will be reintegrated in our society. As you experience the Earth as one global family, you pave the way for balance and fulfillment. You become responsible for yourself by learning to manage your system like a business so you can profit from it, and through example, you teach your children to do the same.

Greet everyone as family. Family is warm and nurturing; it feels good. Family loves without caring what your imperfections are. It doesn't necessarily have to agree with all your choices, but loves, supports and nourishes you to help you make the best choice. Caring for all people, on continually deeper and more sincere levels, is the fastest way for family, businesses, schools, governments, the world, and you, to grow. This degree of family care can only come from going for a deeper heart connection within yourself — and with each individual you meet.

Chapter 18

Deep Heart Listening

After understanding these wider perspectives on holographic DNA blueprints, creation and the family frequency, I realized the ratio of choice each one of us really does have. Feeling a bit overwhelmed by the fantastic complexity of all this, I asked my heart computer: "Could you just simply show me my next level of growth in my personal life." My heart read-out came quickly: "Sara, you can still deep heart listen another level during your daily activities, both to yourself and to others. That will help you integrate all those wide understandings into day-to-day life."

When you really care about something, you do listen deeply and you don't forget much. *Remembering* to deep heart listen while in the thick of activity is real care in action. How can you know your heart directives if you don't listen for them? I saw that self-honesty and honesty with others creates deeper levels of listening.

It didn't surprise me that my heart directed me back to the basics. Deep heart listening is an outstanding tool for loving more sincerely. Everyone wants to *feel understood* in the heart.

It's so important to have someone understand you. If we don't have anyone who can, we feel alone. People often turn to prayer, hoping that God understands. Feeling understood at the heart level is a frequency of hologramatic biology that connects you to the heart of the Creator. We all yearn for that because it's part of our complete DNA blueprint. When we feel understood, we understand more. It's like a switch that activates your DNA template for fulfillment.

In Chapter 8, I explained that deep heart listening involves keeping your energies focused in the heart as you listen. This attunes you to the other person's heart, bringing a more sensitive, essence-based understanding of their frequencies and words. You truly help another *feel cared for* at a heart level.

Communication is always an exchange of frequencies. As you listen to your own heart more deeply, heart intuition magnetizes energy from the *Source* to your system. Then it's your head's job to formulate this energy into words to give you more knowing. The deeper you listen, the deeper meaning you'll gain. The math will be broken down in a geometric sequence to give you a more complete understanding. There's math that covers all the corners and the whole room — from the micro level that can isolate a piece of dust to the macro level that can stand back and see the whole. Deep heart listening can show you both perspectives.

Let's look at the mechanics one more time because

it's important: The heart puts out the intuition, the "wisdom." That's its purpose. Your heart intuition comes through thoughts, images or feelings. The head breaks down the read-out in digits for greater comprehension. It fulfills its most creative function — *to help you decipher intuitive feelings with an explanation, an attitude shift or a different perspective.*

Just ask your heart to help you listen at a deeper level. Tune out your head thoughts and let them go, while you quietly tune to your own heart. Find a peace frequency within your system, wait ten to twenty seconds or more, then listen for a quiet, calm voice or feeling from your heart. Surrender to the common sense or heart intelligence. You will be activating the next program in your DNA for head/heart understanding.

If you practice deep heart listening to yourself during the day, when emotional whirlwinds stir, you have a better chance of not being pulled into the tornado of thoughts. You can intellectually know that everything is frequencies, but when emotional identification is strong, knowledge often goes out the window. I've been in wide bands of understanding, then found myself personally eaten up with an insecurity. Here was a typical example: A friend I admired gave me feedback on my communication and I cringed inside, feeling she didn't like me. "At least I was communicating," I replied, feeling that she'd been too critical. She was deep heart listening and I felt she heard me. Afterwards, however, I found myself in a desperate mental search for the why's and wherefore's. Where could I improve? Why wasn't I more like so-and-so? Why was I shy and uncommunicative? Honest communication can put you in a vulnerable spot, feeling like you're giving your power to someone else. I got over this insecurity by playing a game called "No I.D.," which means you practice having no identification with insecure thoughts and feelings when they pop up. You surrender them to your heart and get a truer perspective.

After putting a control knob on self-identification during communications, I found deep heart listening to personal critiques to be a fun challenge. The "No I.D." game helps balance your emotions so they don't run away with you. As a result, I could hear truth without cringing or feeling hurt. It freed me to feel the sincerity of another and know it was all okay. I no longer had to go through all the mental digits to try to understand my reaction. I could just go directly to the heart, stay in the universal flow and quickly reach a common-sense perspective. I found I crunched time by staying in the heart and letting understanding come to me.

There were still times I chose to let my heart patiently listen to all the head concerns. I would listen with compassion to the hesitation, doubt or fear. As the heart listened deeply, satisfying understandings and solutions followed. But, if my head just wanted to fuss, complain or stack up justified reasoning *and I let it,* no solution came. I felt only frustration, anger and stress. If I let the head take over, rather than holding to the deeper heart, the old insecurities would start up again. I began to see that I only felt insecure when I *identified* with the head hesitations or fears and stopped deep heart listening to my own self.

Deep heart listening keeps unfolding new math. It gets more refined with practice. Don't let your thoughts be colored by past associations or head band distortions. If my head and heart still won't agree on a solution, then my heart lets my head express itself further. Afterwards, I try to keep my head calm and my mind open to hear the heart's response. Whenever my head sincerely listens, heart intelligence brings understanding and unravels solutions to the problem.

A game I play often is realizing my "real teacher" is inside me. When we ignore that real teacher, we create stress. Mind-sets, stubbornness and recycling old problems keep bringing us back to square one and we find ourselves saying, "if only I'd listened to my heart in the first place." It takes practice to be constantly in touch, so be patient with yourself. Don't beat yourself when you forget. Just start deep heart listening again, caring for yourself from that moment. You'll bring your heart back into focus. We all have moments when we get disappointed in ourselves. No one is perfect. Going back to the heart is the most perfect action you can take in any moment. When your holographic picture is out of focus or the sound is distorted, going back to the heart adjusts the film. Then you can continue on with your movie in fun.

LISTENING TO OTHERS MORE SINCERELY

Most of us have vivid memories of conversations where we felt we weren't really being heard. Maybe our words were heard, but not our feelings or real meaning. Remember these times when someone speaks to you and listen to them as you'd like to be listened to. This means *caring* to make sure your own thoughts aren't going a mile-a-minute, which will block you from hearing their essence. Listening is a true art and there's always room for improvement.

As I listen to others, I'm serious about wanting to hear them totally. If I have strong feelings about an issue, it's hard not to make assessments while someone is talking. If I do, I usually miss an important frequency or even misinterpret what they're saying. Deep insights often come to me while I listen to someone. But if I try to hold onto the insight, I miss their entire next sentence or more. Then I have to ask them to repeat what they said and my wonderful insight vanishes anyway. By fully focusing on the other person's essence, words and meaning, I find the insights come back at the right time.

Forming assessments or opinions while people are telling their story is a form of mental interruption. You don't have to agree with what someone is saying but if you wait until they're done speaking before you address your own thoughts, you'll actually have more to offer them. *When people feel heard at the essence level, they connect with their heart.* Often they come up with their own insights because you were loving them and listening deeply. It's a joy to see their face light up when they find their own solution.

There are three essential elements to be aware of while listening: 1. Word Level — what is actually said. 2. Feeling Level — the feelings or frequencies behind the words. 3. Essence Level — the real meaning. Through listening to a person's heart, you can tune to the frequency, the meaning and the words all at the same time. Your intuition is likely to provide a common-sense solution that has both understanding and kindness.

When people come to talk to me, they tell me they often have insights. It's because I'm listening to them sincerely on all three levels with totally focused attention, not because I'm necessarily so intelligent or imparting any pearls of wisdom. I can hear what they are saying between the lines, which makes them *really* feel understood. That's what releases their own heart wisdom. I've found deep heart listening to be a profound system of communication and a tremendous asset at home, at work, anywhere.

Chapter 19

Forgiveness

F orgiveness is one of the ultimate power tools for personal transformation. You do yourself a *huge* favor when you truly let go and forgive. If you make a deep heart contact with yourself *first*, then sincerely forgive yourself or someone else, you receive an extremely high return of peace for your effort. Remember that *anyone* can get off track and make a left-hand turn. Forgiveness is really for you more than them. Often, the people whom you haven't forgiven don't even know it. But your own system does. So do it for yourself rather than waste energy through continual, *often subliminal*, mental and emotional processing.

Forgiveness can seem hard to do when you've been betrayed or deeply hurt. When you feel justified in not forgiving someone, that resentment stays with you and can gnaw away inside for your whole life. Forgiveness from the head just doesn't work! The hurt lurks in the subconscious and resurfaces once a month, once a day, once a night, and for many people, every day and every night. Even if it comes up only once a year, it's still stewing in your subconscious and draining your spirit. If you find yourself saying, "Well, I've forgiven him, but I don't want him in my face," or, "I forgive you but I don't ever want to see you or talk to you again," you haven't forgiven. If your stomach wrenches or you still have a negative association at the mention of a person's name, you haven't truly forgiven.

True forgiveness erases all negative associations from your holographic heart. When you don't forgive and resentment festers, your anger can turn into hate. Let's say you live in Los Angeles and commute through heavy traffic daily. With cars constantly pulling out in front of you and anger rising each day, you can soon find yourself hating. You hate driving to work, you hate all the other drivers, you hate anyone who crosses your path. As anger stacks, hate can become a prominent frequency in your hologram. Hate casts a dark shadow on your whole life. As you hold onto hate, it creates a pinhole in your hologram that can grow into a crack that becomes very hard to mend. Hate is a total inversion of love — hate destroys.

Sometimes we react with anger or hate and know it's just momentary. But if feelings of anger, betrayal and hate linger and constantly replay in your mind, their frequency becomes engraved in your hologram. It then keeps resurfacing as a deep-rooted, unresolved problem. You can't completely forgive and erase these deeply etched patterns until you see all the perspectives of the grid and understand them. But you won't understand them until you make sincere efforts to forgive. It's a catch-22. That's why total forgiveness of deep patterns takes time. Christ understood the importance of releasing, letting go and truly forgiving. Some of his last words were, "Father, forgive them; for they know not what they do." (Luke 23:34)

Your heart will keep bringing up to conscious awareness old unforgiven feelings and memories for you to forgive, release and let go. As you sincerely try to forgive, it helps to remember that mentally and emotionally processing an unforgiven event drains you, just like a car battery gets drained when the door is left open. Resentment maintains a constant, slow leak that can age you prematurely. Regardless of what another person did or didn't do, don't imprison yourself mentally or emotionally. Life goes on. Sincere forgiveness from the heart will release you and release the heart of the person you were hating, whether they are aware of it or not.

I know of two sisters now in their nineties who are still bitter about a family heirloom that one didn't return to the other fifty years ago. There can be so much hatred and bad blood among family members that some don't speak to each other for years. Statistics show that most murders and assaults are family-related. Being able to forgive is a basic core value for family harmony. You can practice forgiving people by taking responsibility to re-balance your inner mental/emotional disturbances and create *inner* harmony first. As the Doc says, "If you realize, in most cases, that *you are the primary beneficiary* when you forgive someone, you will have more incentive to *complete* the act at the *heart* level. Then, everyone wins."

As you practice forgiveness, your heart wisdom might say, "I forgive him. He really didn't realize what he was doing," or, "He might have been doing the best he knew how," or, "I've made mistakes in my life, too. I sure hope people forgave me. I don't want them to be harboring resentment and hate for me." As you forgive others, it helps erase any negative holographic patterns they may hold about you as well. Because we're all interconnected in the heart, forgiveness helps re-create a harmonious flow between yourself and everyone.

Sincere forgiveness isn't colored with expectations that the other person apologize or change. Don't worry whether or not they finally understand you. Love them and release them. Life feeds back truth to people in its own way and its own time — just like it does for you and me. For many years, I resented someone who had rejected me. I really tried to forgive him, but the way he'd treated me just seemed inexcusable. I thought he was a heel — I wouldn't have treated a dog the way he treated people. I tried to forgive him, but felt like I couldn't release my grievance until he understood what he'd done and apologized sincerely. But he didn't and I couldn't shake the deep hurt either. It was like a festering sore that wouldn't heal.

After many years of trying to forgive, I realized that he'd sincerely done the best he knew how. There was really nothing to forgive — he was just being himself. He'd even been trying to help me in his own way. When I saw that, I felt stupid and had to forgive myself for having been blinded by one strong isolated frequency. Having compassion for myself as someone learning and growing, just like him, released me. By totally forgiving the whole situation, I felt a new lease on life. I saw that never again would I create that kind of self-imprisonment.

Most of us still harbor secret resentments. The quickest way out is to make sincere efforts to release those negative frequencies from your system. Replace them with the sincere heart frequency of forgiveness. Do it over and over again until you feel free. You'll know forgiveness is complete when you have a new perception that's not colored by negative associations. Old whisper feelings might occasionally creep in, but your thoughts remind you, "No, I've forgiven him." Just keep releasing and letting go. Your heart will be at peace and you'll have a light, clean feeling once the program is totally erased from your hologram. Until you feel this freedom, keep activating the power tool of forgiveness.

In the heart, people do understand the importance of forgiveness. They know they want to forgive, but it's frustrating when the hurt doesn't go away. Don't look at yourself as a failure if old resentments resurface with a vengeance and take you back into negative thought loops. View this as your system attempting to flush out the old program. Just tell yourself, "That's a deficit." Be seriously sincere with yourself. Don't give up. Freeze-Frame, go back to your heart intelligence, listen for your inner wisdom and, again, feel forgiveness. Each time you do that, you create an asset for yourself. But if you refuel old hostilities, anger, guilt or pain, you just keep on creating deficits.

Personal freedom is knowing how to use heart intelligence to create more internal power. With power, you can exercise your options. It's only your willing permission that justifies a hurt feeling. You hurt yourself far more by holding onto them than by whatever happened to you in the first place. Build your power to forgive. It's not who hurts us or what happens to us, but our response that entraps us, taking away our real freedom. You'll feel a clean heart connection with yourself and others, once you've totally forgiven.

As you develop your heart and internal power by forgiving, managing any tough situation gets easier. A friend of mine had a boss who could be very cutting. Employees never knew when their productivity might be questioned and many quit in disgust. My friend resented the stifling atmosphere and wondered how long she could stand it. Taking the problem to her heart, she saw her boss as a man with a lot of insecurities. She forgave him and that gave her an inner power. She let his cutting remarks go like water off a duck's back, realizing that *no one could take away her inner freedom.* As a result, she was able to speak up for herself and other employees who were too dumbfounded to speak for themselves. She helped the boss see that the employees did care and that his business was in good hands after all.

Most people blame the outer trappings of life, especially other people, for their woes. This robs them of real freedom and totally saps their power. It's forgiving and releasing those inner entrapments that brings us lasting freedom and empowerment.

Chapter 20

The Magnetics of Appreciation

A s I sincerely forgave everyone and every experience that seemed to have any lingering residue, I began to feel an exhilarating sense of freedom. Without all that old junk in the way, life became gorgeous. I appreciated just being *alive*. Instead of always having to recover from some lump or bump, my day-to-day life turned into a fun game of discovery. I discovered the tremendous magnetic power of appreciation and saw the law of magnetics at work: the more I appreciated, that magnetic energy attracted more wonderful people and fulfilling life experiences to appreciate.

The word "appreciation" means to be thankful and express admiration, approval, or gratitude. It also means to grow or appreciate in value. As you appreciate life, you become more valuable — both to yourself and others. Appreciation is what I call a "super power tool" for personal growth and universal evolution. It rapidly shifts your frequencies from head to heart, bringing you a quick attitude adjustment and giving your mission in life a lift. When I began to explore the power of appreciation, I realized that my deepest friendships were the ones I'd appreciated, the ones I valued enough to look after. I also remembered the relationships that had crumbled. They didn't *grow in value* because I didn't appreciate them! The power of appreciation seemed so obvious, but I also knew how often this simple truth gets lost in judgment and insecurity. Appreciating each other is a true family value, one that will bail out much of the stress on the planet and help strengthen the universal bond all people have.

As you value the challenges in your day-to-day life, you begin to see how they are designed for your growth. I found that my sincere effort to appreciate helped me gain more inner control — more power to manage my energy on those "off" days and "off" moments. Appreciation brought me instant heart contact.

One day, I felt the overload of being a single parent. There was so much to take care of: supporting my son and myself, work responsibilities, school, my own growth, and how to balance all of it! It was "one of those days." I wished I could go somewhere to escape. Rent was due and Christian's teacher had sent me a note saying he'd forgotten his homework three times in the previous week. I felt like a failure. I decided to do a Heart Lock-in for five minutes. In the lock-in, I sent appreciation to his teacher for helping him grow, and I realized that even though it was going to be tight this month, we still had a roof over our heads and food on the table. Appreciating gave me a feeling that somehow everything would be okay. When I opened my eyes, there was a co-worker with news that we had just received payment on a large sale I had made — that would take care of the rent. An hour later, Christian's teacher called to say how much better he had been doing in school. It was as if a kaleidoscope had turned — what had been bleak, gray colors were now sparkly, bright hues. Humbled, I appreciated the fact that I am always taken care of. Sometimes it takes a humbling experience to help us appreciate. I appreciated the gift of appreciation itself, and the rest of the day seemed to fall right in place in an almost magical way.

Whenever you activate heart power tools, you open the door to new perceptions. Appreciation is a powerfully magnetic energy that helps you see the wider picture faster. As you appreciate, you see more and understand more. On an energy level, it brings intuitive breakthroughs and helps you realize God is within you. Appreciation magnetizes you to the universal flow. When you sincerely appreciate what you have in life, you magnetize more of your true heart's desires. Mathematically speaking, if people spent half as much time appreciating *what they have* as they do complaining about what they don't have, life would have to get better.

What you put out comes back. You are creating your own world. Appreciation is like looking through a wide-angle lens that lets you see the entire forest, not just the one tree limb you walked up on. In our culture, most people remember negative events more quickly than they do positive ones. Focusing on the negative comes easy to the head, while focusing on the positive comes easy to the heart. When a negative event sends a pain signal to the head, the head tries to figure out how to stop the pain. If it doesn't have an immediate answer, it goes into the analyzing, sorting, processing mode to try to find one. A powerful bailout for a painful event is appreciation. Appreciation is an opening frequency. You receive new intuition when you can sincerely say, "I'll find the good in this situation no matter what. I'll plug in this program from my heart computer — appreciation."

Appreciating something positive in a negative event sends a signal to the heart that magnetizes balanced understanding. Why not remember the positives? They're the fuel for your self-empowerment. It doesn't really matter what you appreciate — as long as it's sincere. The activation of this particular heart frequency is what counts. Appreciate that you have food to eat, a job, your health, a place to sleep instead of the sidewalks, and all the positives you take for granted. Create an *attitude of gratitude* and you'll magnetize more rewarding experiences. As Doc says in *The How to Book of Teen Self Discovery*,

> "Appreciate anything — even if it seems silly. Look around you for something to appreciate. Look at a lamp and appreciate Thomas Edison. Look at the carpet and be glad it's not cement. Look at a chair and be happy you don't have to sit on the floor all the time. Appreciate yourself for trying to appreciate. *Anything* can be appreciated."

As you appreciate in the moment, the magnetics make the returns come back even faster. This gives you more truthful perceptions of events or situations that are unpleasant. Of course tough situations are harder to appreciate. But if you go to the heart, you realize that things could be worse and are worse for a lot of people. It's all a matter of perspective. Find something about a tough situation that you can appreciate. Start by appreciating that no matter what the problem is, there is a wider perspective yet to be uncovered. Don't be afraid of the temporary discomfort. As you look for what you can appreciate, your perceptions shift so that new understandings and solutions can come into your awareness. Have compassion, and appreciate yourself for appreciating, until a solution appears.

My friend Bruce told me recently how powerful the practice of appreciation had been for him. Several years ago he realized that even though he had a good job, a nice place to live, and a wonderful wife and baby, he still had a lot of stress and not much hope it would get better. A conversation with the Doc convinced him to give appreciation a try. He started by appreciating his lunch break — the food, the surroundings, the people — instead of feeling like he had to work right through lunch. What a difference! That started a momentum that helped him see other things in his life he had been taking for granted. His entire holographic heart holodome, his reality, began changing — in real life. He practiced appreciating the loving essence in each person he met and was amazed what a different perspective it put on everything and how much better he felt.

The rewards of appreciation are tremendously increased as you practice with deeper levels of sincerity. If you practice appreciating the little things in life, then when bigger problems or situations arise, you find you have an easier time dealing with them. Appreciation is simply a magnificent feeling in the heart that becomes the compass to find more good. It's the fast track to finding balance and fulfillment.

Chapter 21

Care or Overcare?

Harvard psychologist David McClelland did studies which proved that the feeling of care enhances a person's immune system through increased production of the hormone, salivary IgA, which protects against colds and flu. A clinical study on care-giving among nurses revealed that care is what gives nursing its real meaning; it provides nurses with an over-arching sense of connectedness to all of life. My older sister Sue was a nurse and she has this kind of care. Through caring, true spiritual connectedness can be experienced. It is one of the most regenerative, productive and powerful frequencies for health and well-being. Care is an oil that lubricates the entire mental, emotional and physical system. If you run your system without care, it's like running your car without oil — resulting in friction and breakdown.

Care is another one of those four-letter words, like love, that cages a powerful frequency band. Without care, life grinds metal on metal. True care regenerates both the sender and receiver. It's a nurturing and healing energy. As the Doc says, "Here's a user-friendly recipe for Love: Put a bunch of care in a pot; stir and whip until it starts to thicken; then serve."

Care creates security and support for all involved. It is the cohesive substance that saves a relationship once the initial romance or novelty has worn off. Care is the ingredient that keeps true friendships alive despite separation, distance, or time. Care gives latitude to another person and gets you past the dislikes and annoyances. Quite simply, caring sustains love. When Christian was just a few months old, my mother told me, "Love Christian no matter what because he's your child, your responsibility and no one will love him as much as you will." That was one of the most important things she ever said to me. True care is the family frequency that's missing in the core of people's interactions and involvements all over this world. People's core values often lie dormant within the heart. The practice of loving and caring for people at deeper and more sincere levels will awaken the core values of being.

Care flowing through your system gradually reconnects you with your spirit and vitality. Care enough about yourself to go to your heart to get peace, clarity, and direction before you act. True self-care has to come first. Take a moment and ask yourself two things, "How do I feel when others truly care for me?" and "How do I feel when I care about other people?"

Most of us have had a teacher, a parent, a spouse,

or someone who sincerely cared for us and then suddenly stopped caring. It feels like the rug has been pulled out from under us. One of the most traumatic experiences of my life was like that. The contrast between how nurtured and wonderful I felt when this person deeply cared for me, and how dry and terrible it felt when he stopped, was a shock to my entire system. My heart had opened to him and I felt so secure in his care. When it was no longer there, I felt like I'd fallen off a hundred foot bridge and landed on cement. There was nothing I could do but pick up the pieces and try to care for myself.

Most people have had similar experiences and know what it feels like. Life seems to give us these lessons so we don't totally depend on others for our strength. We have to find it in our own heart instead. Then care from another person is a great gift, but we aren't destroyed if it's not there. Developing your own caring at deeper levels brings an inner security that allows your heart to stay open, regardless of what others do.

When she gives seminars, my friend Debbie often tells a story about her first insight into the power of care. When she was a child, her brother and his wife traveled to Latin America for graduate work. They returned to their home in Nebraska, bringing their maid and her six-year-old son Diego with them. Diego spoke no English and had never been away from the impoverished village where he was born. Debbie had just been given a new bicycle, so she decided to put a fresh coat of paint on her old red bike and give it to Diego. She spent an entire Saturday straightening the fender, painting the bike and attaching a new basket she bought with her allowance. She said that never before had she felt so good in her heart as she did then, knowing she was truly caring for this little boy whom she'd not yet met. Her parents attached the bike to the back of the family car and off they drove to her brother's home 400 miles away. The look of delight on Diego's face and the gratitude that shone from his eyes gave my friend a deep feeling of care in return. It taught her about the power of true care in ways that no Sunday school words ever had.

When I first heard this story, I wondered if something as simple as this, but so potent, could change a destiny. In that "Kodak" moment when Debbie and Diego connected in the heart, could a holographic picture of hope have been etched in their hearts? From Debbie's world, that simple feeling of care was so sincere, it followed her through life.

TRUE CARE VERSUS OVERCARE

From a heart perspective, simply and sincerely sending love to someone is conscious care in action. Suppose, for example, that a close friend is having quite a few bumps and lumps in her life. Since you truly care for her, loving her would be the heart intelligent action to take. But, quite often, when you send love to someone all kinds of thoughts about their situation pop up! If you've focused your energy in the heart, your intuition can facilitate these thought patterns, allowing your Christ-self to help you understand a wider perspective. Your next thoughts could lead you to an intuitive breakthrough on how to help your friend through the difficult time. But if the energies slip into your lower heart frequencies of sentiment and sadness about your friend's difficulties, then in comes the head chatter — the worry and stress. The motivation often starts with care, but in our head-oriented society, it easily slips into overcare.

Care is the essence of service, yet overcare is probably the biggest energy drain and stress producer for teachers, nurses, counselors, environmental and peace workers — people who want to do good for others and the world. Overcare is what leads to burn-out among care-givers in our society. This could explain why psychiatrists have the highest suicide rate in the country.

Parents often think they have to overcare and worry about their children to feel they are really caring for them. This is a terrible misconception. Worry never brings balanced solutions to problems. In fact, most of us recoil from people who are overcaring and worrying about us. Overcare actually blocks the flow of sincere care between the sender and recipient.

On the other hand, there are many people so cut off from their hearts *they don't care at all* and have become numb. There has been a time or two in my life when it seemed so right to care, so important, that I would get stressed out over the outcome and decide it was better not to care at all. That just made things worse. I cut off my own heart and the results were more stressful than caring too much. Both overcare and not enough care create stress and can lead to burn-out.

There are many people who can't work, sleep, or eat because of worrying over someone else's problems. If your care about someone is producing stress, realize it has become overcare. Use your heart computer to know when your concern has become a deficit instead of an asset. As you recognize and understand when your energies slip into overcare, you will see how it's no longer efficient for you or anyone else. Freeze-Frame and go back to your heart for re-direction. Appreciate that at least you did care and have compassion for yourself. Overcare is just a third dimensional human inversion of care. Don't get confused. We all have some overcare to deal with because we're all living in a stressful third dimensional world. It's easy to feel like a tightrope walker in the middle of a three-ring circus.

If care is oil for your system, then overcare is an oil leak. Whether you're troubled over small things or over big things like the world situation, the principle of how to deal with them is the same. Go back to your heart and re-start. If you're sitting at home just worrying about someone or worrying about the global stress report on the evening news, you aren't doing anyone any good. Most importantly, you are harming yourself. Overcare will drain you, physically, emotionally, mentally and spiritually.

Overcare about the environment used to bleed my energies away and cause a huge deficit in my personal energy account. I worried about all the Styrofoam and baby diapers that would not disintegrate — and the nuclear waste. I worried about the wildlife that is becoming extinct. Christian has a deep affection for birds and animals. He has told me the names of many that are fast disappearing from the earth. Some people dedicate their entire lives to these problems. I care, and I wanted to understand what my purpose was relative to these concerns. My heart gave me this insight: It's possible that without enough *care for each other*, so much irreparable damage in the collective holographic heart of humankind would be created that *our own species could become extinct*. I realized that by sending sincere focused heart to people and environmental issues, I was doing more to help the planet than draining my energy worrying whether it was efficient for me to recycle all my aluminum cans and bottles. Letting go of the worry didn't mean I buried my head in the sand and ignored the problem. I began to use my heart computer to make balanced decisions. I took the issues just as seriously but didn't allow them to drain my power. I chose to do what felt right in my heart and felt best for the whole. Heart-directed care broadens your awareness and gives you balanced answers that are best for everyone.

Overcare can be caused by right motives — real care — taken to inefficient extremes. It can also be caused by wrong motives, like worrying if someone is going to get a better job, car, or bonus than you. Ambition, competition and expectancy are all examples of overcare motivated by the head. Stress rules the planet and overcare is one of its field generals in disguise. The planet is starving for true, balanced care.

The bottom line is that overcare in any disguise is simply not energy-efficient. When you recognize it in your thoughts and feelings, remind yourself to Freeze-Frame and go back to your heart for re-direction. Self-adjust. By following your heart intelligence, overcare energy transmutes naturally into true care. Not even the animals need become extinct if we care. Don't hurt yourself with overcare, but do care.

GLOBAL CARE

The entire world is undergoing tremendous change and growth at this time. As does a teenager going through adolescence, the planet needs a lot of care. Earth was created in the beginning as a planet of love and care. That's obvious to anyone who looks at the beauty of nature. It's a family planet. If we look from the perspective of a caring mother, Mother Earth would want to help her children grow up with as few scratches and scrapes as possible. But there's a fine balance to parenting. In caring for your child, how much do you protect him and how much do you let him explore and make his own mistakes? When your child is learning to walk, you let him fall down and pick himself up. He'd never learn to walk if you didn't let him do it himself. If he scrapes his knee, you comfort him and put on a band-aid. Then you let him try again. A mother wouldn't take away the experience of the scrape because she knows that's how he'll learn, gain his security and become independent. She wants her child to grow up and be responsible for himself.

As I described earlier, the human family as a whole is moving into a new hologram. In this transition over the next ten to twenty years, everyone will have the chance to *choose to love and care* — the passwords to entering the new holographic reality. Those who are not ready will find themselves in another reality, on another third dimensional family planet, where they can continue to grow and learn to care at their own pace. Mother Earth would rather not lose even one of the souls that are part of her body. But, like any truly caring mother, she would rather they be where they can learn what they need to learn than overcare that they won't be part of her immediate family any longer. It is possible, if enough people move forward in the choice to care, that we can create a network of love and light so finely woven that not one soul need be left behind. The magnetics of such a grid would awaken the hearts and minds of all people to the understanding that to love and care is the only common sense choice.

Chapter 22

Death –
A New Frontier

When we talk about global change, it's natural to feel a moment of overcare about how events may unfold. In many life situations, your heart will tell you to take some action or make a change, and you have the power to do so. But then there are the events in life that we have little or no power to change. For example: a job lay-off, the death of someone close to you, a hurricane, or an earthquake. You can't stop these events from happening, but you can control the way you deal with them — from the heart or from the head. Let's talk about death, an event over which we seem to have no control.

Our culture appears death-ridden. Death, in some form or another, is frequently the major news in media reports — wars, fire, famine, AIDS, car crashes, natural disasters, famous people who die, and the list goes on. Many people religiously read the newspaper obituary columns every day. On the other hand, our own death is a theme that most of us zealously try to avoid. People don't much like to talk about it. We mention it in whispers or hushed tones, if at all. Our society requires that all possible medical means be employed to keep a person alive, even at immense cost in money, suffering, and energy. In other words: Do anything but die, because that means the end. This overall social perspective reflects how little we know about death, so our desire is to ignore the whole unpleasant subject.

Conditioned by the heightened materialism of our time, people tend to see themselves as just physical bodies. Inspite of religious beliefs in life after death, the idea that we are only physical matter has kept people in bondage to pain, sorrow, suffering and death for thousands of years. "Ashes to ashes and dust to dust...," as they say at most funerals. In his book *Life after Life**, psychiatrist Raymond Moody describes his thorough investigation of life after death experiences, concluding we are more than our physical bodies and we do go on after death. Dr. Elizabeth Kubler-Ross conducted similar research and confirmed Moody's findings.

Eight million Americans, one adult in twenty, have reported life after death experiences in which they saw themselves leave the body. Many could see their bodies still on the operating table, with doctors and nurses struggling to revive them. Many also reported traveling at great speeds toward a brilliant light. All were clinically dead, their hearts had stopped beating, but they came back to life. Clinically, because the heart could not send blood to the brain, many should have suffered brain damage, but did not. These survivors were able to describe exact details of the actions and conversa-

* Raymond Moody, Jr., *Life after Life*, (Bantam, 1988)

tions of the people around their "dead" body. Scientists, at a loss for a logical explanation, have attempted to explain these experiences as hallucinations caused by a lack of oxygen to the brain. But, if these "dead" people were able to observe and, later, accurately describe in detail what was happening to their body and to the people in the same room with their body, then by what means were they hearing and viewing the scene? Certainly not through their physical ears and eyes!

These statistics do not even include the thousands of documented cases of clinically dead children who also reported similar experiences. In their recent book, *Closer to the Light: Learning from the Near Death Experiences of Children** (recently on the NEW YORK TIMES bestseller list for months), Melvin Morse and Paul Perry describe careful research done with children who died and then came back to life. Dr. Kenneth Ring, president of the International Association for Near-Death Studies, believes "such experiences, as well as death itself, are really nothing more than the shifting of a person's consciousness from one level of the hologram of reality to another."

All this evidence provides an increasingly solid basis to conclude that the soul continues and is very much alive after the body dies. Even a partial understanding of these views of the "other side" serves to mitigate the fear of death, which is due to third dimensional ignorance and uncertainty about conscious survival after the body dies.

Modern media has brought to light many wonderful clues to the realms of experience after death. Even the experience of watching a movie is like being in an-

* Melvin Morse and Paul Perry, *Closer to the Light*, (GK Hall, 1991)

other world. When you go to the movies, you see projected in sound and light what looks like bodies walking around, but they're not real, they're images. Intellectually, you know that frequencies of sound and light are creating an illusion, that light is passing through film and being projected onto a screen. Yet, while you are absorbed in the movie, it all seems real. Death is like moving into another movie, a new holographic film.

Think of your body as a shell that houses your spirit. A friend of mine used to keep hermit crabs as pets. She enjoyed watching a hermit crab leave his shell, still alive and well, and sort through the other colorful shells in the terrarium to find a new home. She also told me about an experience that stayed with her all her life. When she was four years old her grandfather died — her first experience with death. She was lying in bed on the night of the funeral, wondering if death was really final — the end — as her brother had said. At that point she suddenly saw a total stark blackness inside, blacker than any black she had ever seen. It had a feeling of "being final," yet... "there was some kind of unseen light there as well." The shock scared her a bit and she decided to forget about it, and just enjoy life. But she never forgot it.

When I was five years old, my family and I drove cross-country, moving from one military base to another. On the trip I became very dehydrated and sick with a terribly high temperature and was rushed to the hospital. I went into kind of a dream where I saw everyone running around nervous and worried, then suddenly happy and at ease again. Then I experienced a transitioning of the body into a freer realm. Looking back on it now, it seemed like a place where souls can blend and merge so that consciousness becomes one even while a sense of personal identity is retained. The experience of the ecstasy of love was intense. I felt like I was myself, but also felt embraced in a circle of my family's arms. Everything seemed so much brighter and lighter, as if everything was smiling. It was a tremendous experience. Next, I remember riding on a stream of light, and on the shore was everyone in my family. It was like a picnic, or a birthday party, and I realized everything was all right. Later, when I woke up in my hospital bed, my parents told me the doctors and nurses thought they were going to lose me.

There are many accounts of people who've lost close relatives and feel very strongly that their deceased loved ones telepathically communicate with them, comfort them, and at times appear to them in an etheric or spiritual body. In a Heart Smarts™ seminar one of my associates gave for a group of public school teachers, she mentioned that, in the heart, some people talk to their deceased relatives. One of the teachers spoke up and said that she and her dead mother often converse in the heart and she finds it very natural. My associate was surprised when over half the people in the room said they had communicated with departed relatives but were afraid to tell anyone.

I made peace with death at an early age, but that doesn't mean I might not have a bit of anxiety and wonderment if I knew I were going to die next week. After all, isn't death a separation from your emotions and thoughts as you know them, as well as a separation from your vital parts? I now understand death to be a separation or disconnection that's quite similar to sleep. Sleep could be seen as a rehearsal for dying. During sleep, you are often somewhere else. As I drifted off to sleep as a child, I felt at home traveling to new places and gaining new understandings of the dimensions I explored. At times, when I watch Christian sleep at night, I can see his face change from quizzical to intense with a furrowed brow, to smiling in his sleep. He's obviously somewhere else behind those closed eyes.

I've never felt totally responsible for what I was doing in a dream, but whatever I did certainly could influence my day-to-day world. I don't remember dreams very often. It's as though my awareness on the dream level is erased before coming back to the waking state of the third dimension. You might ask, "What about nightmares?" Like many people, I've had frustrating nightmares in which I was trying to escape something or someone but couldn't, or was caught in a struggle that never seemed to end. I see this as a process of slowing down frequencies and giving them certain recognizable forms in order to work something out.

There were times my nightmares went on for days. I could see them as releasing the leftovers of old programs in a form I call "sidejunk." These were patterns that I no longer really identified with in daily life, patterns I no longer required for my growth but were still there as residue. Nightmares can feel and seem so solid and real, that I look at them the same way I would look at a conscious negative thought. I Freeze-Frame the experience, then release its negative residue rather than add more negative energy to it. By viewing a nightmare as some pattern being worked out or released and let-

ting it go, you can understand and consciously eliminate the pattern. Many people believe you need to analyze your dreams and nightmares to gain understanding. Nightmares can have intrigue, but analysis of them
tends to over-activate the head bands and add to your
discomfort. Through the heart, you gain the understanding you want, release the pattern and move on. Nightmares could be part of a holographic prenatal blueprint
of yours, or part of a holographic blueprint of the mass
consciousness on earth. Often they are a translation of
vibrations into images of lower states of consciousness.

Many people view nightmares and death as terrible or wrong, or as a sign of failure. People know they'll
die someday, but still look at death as something they
never want to do. This aversion runs like a constant
thread through their lives. From a heart computer perspective, death just means it's time to move on. It's not
the end. It's just discarding your shell, the end of a chapter in your book. Thankfully, it's also the end of your
pain, the end of your fear, and the end of your frustrations in life. At the right time and in the right attitude,
death can be an exhilarating experience. Death in itself
is not really problematic. It's just a big mystery to people.

The fear of the unknown drives us to look for a
solid physical reality to hold onto for security. Your head
can't release your worse nightmares or your fears about
death. Thoughts of dying can process through the head,
with fear tagging along, and then escalate to such an
extent that they become a huge stress burden that people
carry through life. Many worry, "Will I suffer?" "Will I
have prolonged disease?" "Will death be painful?"
Death is inevitable. A sense of security about death can

only be found in your own heart. Your heart intelligence understands death. The timing, conditions, and method of death are determined by your holographic DNA blueprint. When you become conscious of that, you can choose to be fully aware when the moment of death comes. It can be a joyous transition into a new life.

MOURNING

If your partner or someone close to you dies, there obviously will be a feeling of loss. Take this feeling to your heart intelligence. Your heart will help you understand that you do not necessarily need to feel sad for them. Death might be for their highest best. If this is the case, then the real reason you are sad is because they left you or left their family. It's best to accept that they really are never coming back and that you're not absolutely sure where they're going either. From a truthful perspective, what you are mourning is your own loss.

It's important not to deny grief and mourning. Repression of these vulnerable feelings will not bring the release you need. Don't drag grief around with you for a year or two. As I said before, it does you no good and just creates a stress burden when you hold on to loved ones who've gone on. Let the deceased go. As illogical as it can seem, realize they are never just victims of external conditions. It's likely they chose in their blueprint to go on, consciously or unconsciously, for reasons known only to their soul.

THE OTHER SIDE

We hear accounts quite often of communications between those who have died and those still living.

People go to mediums and channelers hoping to speak to a deceased loved one. Radio talk show host Joel Martin wrote a best-selling book about the famous channeler George Anderson and his conversations with the other side. Martin had set out to expose and debunk Anderson, but because Anderson knew intimate details about Martin's life and the lives of others that no one could have possibly known except from the deceased, Martin wrote a book about it instead.

A friend of mine was in the bank one day when a teller told her about the death of a mutual friend, named Jack. Jack and his whole family died when their small plane crashed into a mountain shrouded by fog. My friend was stunned. Later, in her prayers she saw Jack smiling and content. He asked her to call his mother and tell her that he was very happy. My friend had never done anything like this before. She had never spoken with Jack's parents, but found a number in the telephone book. When she called, a man answered the phone. She asked if he was the father of Jack. When he said yes, she told him what she'd experienced. The man began to cry. He told her that his son's real mother had died when he was quite young, but that he'd been extremely close to his stepmother. He thanked her deeply for calling and said it would mean a great deal to his wife.

Death can be an extremely stressful time for loved ones left behind, but using heart power tools can help all concerned understand and release grief more quickly so you and they can move on. In the holographic universe no one is ever lost to you. In fact, their connection to your heart becomes easier from the multi-dimensional worlds of heaven. Always remembering the one who has died with appreciation and love helps you feel that continuity of heart connection.

Some people are so totally identified with the body structure and the materialistic world, they have a harder time moving on after death. They cannot easily detach from the physical body and get caught in an in-between place called the astral world. They try to re-enter the physical world, hang around their old house, watch their children play, and try to interact with this third dimensional hologram. But they can't. They don't have bodies and no one can see them or hear them. Astral beings are responsible for much of the poltergeist phenomena you read about or see dramatized in movies. They are the ghosts who rattle tables to gain attention. Caught between worlds, these entities often have frustrating and horrifying experiences.

A dear friend of mine, Katie, lost her father when she was a teenager. He was reported Missing In Action while serving in Vietnam. About two years later, the family began to experience poltergeist phenomena around the house. Water would suddenly turn on in the bathroom. The bed would shake in the middle of the night, and chairs would fall down for no reason. The family was terrified. Whenever my friend came back from a date, the phenomena would get noisier. It was as if someone was trying to run the family. The disturbances continued year after year. Katie and her mother both suspected that the ghost was her father. Knowing that I see energy fields quite easily, Katie's mother asked me if I would try to communicate with him and find out what was going on. I said I would try.

I went over to the house and walked around to get a feel for the situation. I did a Heart Lock-in and sent love to Katie's father. Soon I felt myself in the presence of a very disturbed being. I was able to connect with a frequency where we established clear telepathic communication. The first thing he asked me was to give a message to "Kit-Kat." I didn't know it, but that had been his nickname for Katie. There was other verification that helped Katie and her mother know that it really was Katie's father. I tried to explain to him that he was dead and needed to move on. Being in the astral world it was hard for him to accept that when he evidently felt alive. I had tremendous compassion for him. Obviously he didn't understand death. He told me that he thought he was supposed to stay there and take care of his family. He'd said he'd been shot down and hurt in Vietnam, and thought he was just continuing on with life. Beings had tried to approach him to ask him to move on and come with them, but he was terrified and wouldn't go. He felt he belonged with his family. With a lot of love, care and heart from all of us, he chose to try to go on. He had been in that disoriented state for more than twenty years. When I saw Katie a month later, she thanked me and said, "I feel my father's at peace and our house is at peace."

My experience with Katie's father started me wondering what "judgment day" was all about. My heart computer showed me that what is called judgment day is just your own review of your holographic filmstrips. You see what you did in life, and then decide what sort of learning experience, or "job," you would like next. It's nothing to be afraid of. People fear judgment day because, at an unconscious level, they fear re-experiencing the filmstrips of the left-hand turns they have taken in life.

For several years, my friend Frankie had been suffering from lupus, a form of cancer. She bore it gracefully with a childlike spirit, but when she lay dying, she fought her oncoming death. Several friends and I went to see her to gently encourage her to let go and move on, assuring her it was okay. She was scared by a feeling that she hadn't completed something here on earth. But the more she held on, the worse she got. She developed gangrene and her pain increased. She couldn't find any inner comfort. One day, a friend and I sat by her bedside and just sent heart to her. After a while, we both dozed off. The next thing we knew, we heard her say, "Oh, an angel." Both of us opened our eyes at the same time and saw her reaching toward an invisible angel. The next night she died.

As I developed more intuition, receiving more isolated frequencies from my holographic heart patterns, I came to certain understandings. I realized that since there is no real death and the soul goes on, we all have had many past "life" times. Past lives don't determine this lifetime, even though they can influence it. It's a matter of "karmic choice," not what people call "karmic law." Karma is to eastern religions what sin is to western religions. The concept of both karma and sin is that if you've taken a left-hand turn you have to pay for it. In truth, left-hand turns at any time are only lessons for growth and expansion.

TIME IS AN ILLUSION

Quantum physics has basically destroyed the concept that "cause and effect" are an absolute law. While Newton's law of physics says that, "Every action has an equal and opposite reaction," from the higher fourth dimension that law changes. The action is understood and released through the heart. Quantum physicists have theorized and proven that time is an "illusion," that it's actually possible for a cause to happen at the same time as an effect, or even after. It all depends on which holographic filmstrip you are in, from which angle you are viewing it, and what kind of new filmstrip you are creating as you do this.

Time can be seen as multi-dimensional. From the third dimension, time is linear and therefore cause must come before effect. From the higher fourth dimension, everything is relative to perspective, so it's all one and everything is happening at the same time. From the fifth dimension, since everything is happening simultaneously, you can move in and out of time, enter into different holographic films, and experience the effect before the cause as a real time reality.

So what is time? Maybe nothing more than a convenience we have created for ourselves and then imprisoned ourselves inside of. I do have a great appreciation for time. I can recall my father saying, "Be ready at eighteen hundred hours!" There is a natural respect for time in the military and throughout our social structures. We use it to create efficient connections for people, places, and things in life. It helps keep things orderly. In my conscious effort to be thankful for time, I've expanded my perception of time. I've also lost my former anxiety that time was passing too quickly and the feeling that there was never enough time. I've developed a serene sense of the moment and of the moments to come. Realize that *now*, in this moment of time, you are creating. You are creating your next moment. That is what's real.

In the holographic heart you can discover your past and future lifetimes. These lifetimes do influence each other, just as you and your child, best friend, or husband, influence each other. Moments of time influence each other through our memory of them. Memory is the influence, not time. Since time is an illusion, past, present, and future lifetimes are simultaneous. They all would seemingly be in the same space as you, just in different times. Remember, it's all one big, fluctuating, holographic soup. You are choosing to be conscious of the part you are playing now in the present time, and this is where you should be.

PAST LIVES

A past lifetime reading can have a positive, efficient effect on some people. For others, it can be a detour. For example, remembering and experiencing that you've died many times before could possibly help you release some fear of death. Recalling past lives can also release people from other deep, unconscious fears that they're holding in their current physical body on holographic cellular levels. In this case, the past life memory was so strong that it became imprinted in the DNA blueprint of their present body. Sometimes, through past life recall, a light of new understanding can be turned on.

However, for many people, the glitter of past life readings or predictions becomes a detour. It turns into an excuse *not* to change inefficient patterns in this lifetime. They identify with and become englamored by the past life drama and ignore what they are here to learn now. If their past life experience was problematic, their identification with that pattern often re-creates the same problem in this lifetime.

After my first experience of a past life reading, I came to the conclusion that loving people, places, and things in the moment, seemed to more easily erase my instinctive distaste for certain things in my life today. Whether that distaste was influenced by a past life experience or not didn't matter. What mattered was that love automatically released me from distasteful residues that were coloring and hindering my world.

PARALLEL LIVES

It's possible that there are also parallel lifetimes. In the holographic awareness, I saw that the decision of the spirit to come into a material body was often made before one life ends and the other begins. In other words, the last years of an elderly person's life and the first years of their next life could have the same spirit but in different percentages. You could actually be a five year-old and a ninety year-old at the same time.

Einstein proved mathematically that time is an illusion. By moving into the holographic awareness that Einstein was sensing, it would be possible to experience overlapping lifetimes within the same spectrum of time. This could mean there is another you in the same (time) spectrum, but not in the same space. It would be quite a surprise to meet that other you and have those two time continuums converge, but it's possible as you develop awareness. Movies about time travel, such as *Back to the Future*, and movies about the other side, such as *Defending your Life*, *Ghost*, and the popular TV series *Quantum Leap*, are helping to open people's minds to the higher dimensional perspectives.

Past lives, future lives, this life — our higher intelligence selects what we will experience as an opportunity to grow. Death is never the end of the process. It is the translation of matter back into energy and the soul goes on. Gaining a balanced understanding of death was just another puzzle piece of life coming together that gave me more heart power to make any moment of my day lighter. An understanding of death is available to you in your own heart. If you are frightened or have a strong hesitation about your own death or the death of another, ask for help to deal with this transition. That would be using your heart intelligence.

"Yea, though I walk through the valley of the shadow of death, I will fear no evil: for thou art with me." (Psalm 23:4)

Chapter 23

Balance
(Faster Than Light)

B alance is like standing in the middle of a seesaw and finding how much weight to put on each side so it won't tip over and you can enjoy the ride. Balance applies to all aspects of life — physical, mental, emotional, spiritual. Letting your heart computer weigh the pluses and minuses in each situation is the most efficient means of finding balance.

THE BUSINESS OF BALANCE

Because the heart knows which energy expenditures are efficient and non-efficient, its intelligence can manage your personal assets and deficits. When businesses keep financial records, they use a balance sheet — a record of their assets and liabilities — to determine their bottom line. Most of us know we need to balance our checkbooks to keep track of our cash flow. People who play the stock market pay close attention to the various aspects of their portfolio, maneuvering their assets to create capital gains. This translates into buying power, which in most people's minds represents less stress and more security. Much time and energy is put into evaluating finances. If people put even a small percentage of their time towards balancing their energy expenditures from the heart, what would that do for their real bottom line — peace and inner security?

Have you ever really wanted to do something but found yourself dragging and saying in despair, "I just don't have the energy anymore!"? If people could invest in this kind of vital energy like they can blue chip stocks, it would sell like hotcakes. Life is an economy game. Heart intelligence shows you how to both save and invest your energy efficiently.

KEEPING A PERSONAL BALANCE SHEET

An efficient self-management strategy would be to observe your mental and emotional energy expenditures. If you are serious about wanting a larger return on your energy investments, create a personal balance sheet to see how you spend your precious vital energy, your "vitality." In practicing the HeartMath system, I've often asked my heart computer, "Are my energy expenditures (actions, reactions, thoughts, etc.) productive or non-productive? During the course of my day, have I accumulated more stress or more peace?" Before you go to bed at night, or at some convenient time during your day, try to remember the flow and feeling of your day — its ups and downs and how you felt by the end of it. Truthfully, ask yourself if these feelings added to the quality of your day or detracted from it.

Create a simple form which has an assets column and a deficits column. In the assets column, list events, interactions, and inner dialogues that felt good and efficient to you — not just something that felt good in the moment, but wasn't best for your overall growth. In the deficits column, list events, irritations, frustrations, anxieties, etc., that you know were not wise investments. Assign values to your assets and deficits according to your heart computer read-out, then total up the numbers in each column. Did you have more assets or deficits? Were you efficient in the expenditures of your vital energy? Did they add to the quality and fulfillment of your life or add to your stress accumulation? Looking at the bottom line, you can tell if this was a good day or not. Use your heart computer to make adjustments so you can increase your asset total and make your bad days better and your good days great.

Though it may seem a bit time-consuming to keep a written record of your energy assets and deficits, it will buy time for you in the long run. As you practice, it gets easier and you'll no longer need to write everything down. You'll be able to recognize assets and deficits just by using your intuition. Within time, you'll see where to simply self-correct right in the moment of the day. Remember, you wake up each morning with a specific amount of mental, emotional and physical energy to spend that day. Efficient choices add to your energy account. Inefficient choices deplete your vitality.

Being unaware of energy deficits creates the constant level of stress we as a society have grown accustomed to living in. The huge national budget deficit is a reflection of our individual deficit spending. Learning how to be efficient with your energy expenditures is a heart intelligent way to love yourself and is a cornerstone of self-empowerment. Keeping an energy efficiency balance sheet for yourself is a high-yield investment on the Self-Empowerment Stock Exchange.

ACHIEVING BALANCE

Balancing is an "understanding game" you play with yourself to find out which choices are best for you at any moment in each area of your life. If you manage your head thoughts and emotions enough to see and understand both sides of any issue — both sides of the seesaw — then the balance point is easily accessed. But your head can fool you without an injection of real wisdom from the heart.

It's important to learn the difference between emotional pulls and true heart's desires. I often thought I listened to both sides of an issue. I'd go back and forth analyzing the variables, trying to choose which direction to go. "Should I spend money on a vacation?" or "Should I invest in this stock?" Often, I found myself choosing what I was attached to because of the emotional pull. I thought it was what my heart wanted. Then it wouldn't turn out to be fulfilling or profitable at all. When I learned how to stop the head thoughts by Freeze-Framing and going to the heart computer, I could distinguish the emotional impulse from my real heart and gain a balanced perspective. Quite often, what my heart wanted was not the same as my emotional pull. If my head still had doubts, I would explore the variables, but always using my heart computer as a guide. I learned that good business deals are made when you can see all perspectives.

You probably know many people who rationalize

their emotional pulls. Here's a simple example to illustrate how balance can bring us more fulfillment. A man eats ice cream every day, telling himself it's okay because he works out in the gym an hour every day. That could seemed balanced, but when you look at the amount of ice cream he consumes in proportion to other foods it might come up on the computer screen as an extreme imbalance. If he ate ice cream twice a week, instead of daily, he might discover that he enjoys it even more. It would be up to him to find his true balance point. Balance does not mean you have to live a boring deprived life, never venturing off the middle of the road. Balance is actually the means by which one can more fully savor what life has to offer.

Bringing anything into harmonious proportion increases your overall enjoyment and feeling of well-being. Anything that becomes an addiction is out of balance, whether it's food, alcohol, sex, work, or other stimuli. When balanced by your own self-management, you can appreciate stimulation without losing control.

Passion is a powerfully regenerative energy that is balanced when expressed from the heart. When expressed through the head, passion gets out of balance and can run you around the block, and then some! *It's up to each individual to discover the right balance for their system.* Your own heart computer will indicate areas you need to adjust. You may hear the voice of your conscience inside or have a funny feeling when you begin to do something that will take you out of balance. Stress is a sure sign you're not balanced. As you practice becoming aware of stress, you can then go back to your heart for a read-out on what you might be overdoing, or underdoing, or missing altogether.

SPIRITUAL BALANCE

Spiritual balance comes from having the proper integration and function of the physical, mental and emotional aspects of your life. The spiritual aspect is always there and always has been. It's all spiritual when you make efforts to bring those three levels into harmonious arrangement. Then the spiritual balance you're looking for will come automatically. In fact, if you overcare about your spiritual destiny and ambitions and aren't responsible for these basics, you will be out of balance and hold back your spiritual growth. You won't be as loving or caring or radiate as much heart energy as many people who have no intentional spiritual goals, yet are balanced physically, emotionally, and mentally. These are the people who just love and appreciate life. They are the ones *living* the core values. It could be the person down the block, the grocery store clerk, or even someone you may have judged for being, eating, dressing or acting differently from you. There are no universal formulas for balance applicable to everyone, because everyone is different and everyone's system is different. What counts is not the outer garb or personal habits, but the quality of a person's love that comes from balancing the different aspects of their life.

Many people with ardent spiritual aspirations lack balance. They may pray or meditate all day, but if their system is not truly balanced they will feel they're not advancing. Often they don't know why, so they strive even harder in their spiritual practices. If they truly listened to their heart, their inner voice would tell them where they need to make some adjustments in life. But often, even experienced meditators don't listen to or act on the truth in their hearts.

One of the editors of this book shared with me how finally understanding balance was a major break-through for her. Before she practiced HeartMath, she meditated deeply on the "third eye," having been told that intuition comes from there. But she ignored some of the niggling little voices in her heart because she didn't realize they were the real intuition speaking. She wondered how she could find the fulfillment her heart was yearning for, as she didn't know how to resolve several deep inner conflicts.

Exhausted from the cycle of clearing, then creating more problems to clear, she sincerely asked God for help. When she met Doc Lew Childre, myself and several other friends and saw the balance and care in our lives, she realized this was the missing piece to her puzzle. To her, we were living testimonies that managing life from the heart was possible. She told me what an awakening it was to realize there were actually people on earth achieving high spiritual awareness who were also down-to-earth, responsible, fun-loving — and experiencing fulfillment in life. She was excited about HeartMath and really walking her talk — applying what we'd discovered to her own life.

She started to listen to and follow her heart direc-tives as diligently as she'd practiced her other spiritual disciplines. She found it liberating to put everything through her heart computer. She told me, "I didn't think I *had* mind-sets but I started seeing where I was hold-ing back my progress by 'knowing what I know' about people and situations in life." As she practiced, she started finding balance in ways that surprised her — physically, emotionally, mentally, and of course, spiritually.

Her biggest realization of all was that she didn't have to strive and strain to reach new levels of spiritual awareness. They were a natural result of practicing deeper, more sincere levels of love, care and appreciation for people, all people. She summed it up like this: "How wonderful it is to *finally* just love and care more deeply and sincerely from the heart, and let the spiritual awakenings come to you. They come faster once you start to greet all people from the heart and truly live each moment in balance. With each new level of balance the rewards seem to increase exponentially!"

THE SPEED OF BALANCE

Any family, group, or business will function "powerfully" when it is made up of self-responsible individuals. The same is true of any society, country, or the world. Your heart has the power to take responsibility for manifesting peace and happiness and helping your children do the same. When Christian gets over-amped in playing, I can sense he's out of balance. If I don't remind him right then to slow down and get back in his heart, he can unknowingly step on another child's feelings. To help him remember, I ask him to check his own heart computer — what is its truth?

Remembering to balance your account causes rapid acceleration. HeartMath shows that 1 sincere heart effort — 1 investment in activating heart frequencies — brings a 9 in energy return. A great investment! As you come to know the deeper levels of your own heart, you also come to know that life really boils down to an economy game. As your assets increase, fulfillment increases. As you become more efficient with your mental and emotional energies, you realize that you're winning at the game of life that day, month, or year.

In gaining heart balance, you are going back to your original state. If the real purpose of life is to "Meet your Maker," so to speak, then re-creating and balancing your system would be the means to the end. With "God's" intelligence, or higher heart logic, wouldn't the fastest speed to get back home, reach divinity, be one with the source, or whatever you want to call it, be balance? The straight and narrow path, calculated from your heart computer, is balance!

Is it possible that the equation to take you home is faster than the speed of light? Is it possible that this "faster-than-light" travel (FTL) is actually the <u>speed of balance?</u> As Stanford physicist Nick Herbert, author of the book *Faster Than Light: A Journey Beyond the Einstein Limit** says, "Einstein's theory does not necessarily rule out faster-than-light (FTL) travel." He further says that faster-than-light travel can explain the quantum connection — "the notion that once two quantum systems have briefly interacted, they remain in some sense forever connected by an instantaneous link....unlimited by distance." My experience is that at the speed of light there is a transition into another dimension where everything disappears into energy and there is no space or time. All connectedness exists and everything moves as a wholeness. At that point it's as if the observer has quantized, subdivided into small, finite

---

* Nick Herbert, *Quantum Reality* (Doubleday, 1985), *Faster Than Light* (NAL/Dutton, 1988)

increments of energy. If God is observing from everywhere, and it is from God's infinite perspective that you are looking, then you might see balance as a faster form of travel than the speed of light.

Einstein had the ability to imagine himself traveling on a beam of light and formulated his now famous equation $E=mc^2$ which basically says that energy and matter are the same thing. The next step for science is to become comfortable with $E=mc^2$ as an equation that can also prove energy moves "matter." Let me explain. If "E" is coherent heart energy, and "m" (mass) includes mental and emotional frequencies (thought matters), then "E" would have the ability to balance and change "m." Only through practice can we see how focused heart energy, heart intelligence, can balance external situations and transform density (life's hologram) to a degree previously unrecognized.* This understanding of the <u>speed of balance</u> could exceed all the previous insights spawned by $E=mc^2$. Now, what would $E=(mc^2)^2$ look like? In Einstein mechanics it could be an incredible explosion that would annihilate all matter. But in this wider perspective it might be an explosion in the heart of light, love, and power, releasing consciousness into a new reality. It might be seeing as God sees. This would be reaching past the fourth dimensional perception, where energy equals matter and the speed of light is at a ceiling, and into the fifth dimension. It would give people the power to create in harmony and balance with God.

In the creation frequency there is also future and past, meaning that it would be possible to understand your Creator, His/Her intentions and where He/She came from.

---

* This is explained in detail in *Quantum Intelligence: The Speed of Balance* by Doc Lew Childre. (Available Fall '93. Planetary Publications)

The creation frequency could possibly be the highest frequency capacity that your DNA cells would unfold, a God perspective, a gift of Himself. This would be the unfoldment of the Golden Mean ratio — the unfoldment of Love. Even most religions agree that Love is God's particular purpose. Science will prove that love *is* at the core of the matter through understanding the speed of balance.

You can start now. The Golden Mean Ratio unfolds at the Speed of Balance! This is my experience of how you access it: Through your heart, do your best to find balance in each moment. Then go for deeper, more sincere love and care. For example, when daily life starts to look overwhelming, the first rule in my system is to stay in peace. Then I can find my balance and know what action to take as I follow that flow. I can watch an intricate timing of events where everything seems to fall in place. Since there is no time in reality, balance crunches time into a flow. Everything gets done. You find you are creating your own timing with efficient decisions each moment. As you do your best to balance, it mathematically activates your next level of awareness, so you can enjoy any ride through life and create your next level of fulfillment. Take time to appreciate that. You are creating your own unfoldment, your own spiral of growth. At each step of the way, go back to the heart and balance again. Find your peace. Balance takes you to your next level, and your next, and it goes on in a fun adventure. Balance is like exploring the "Rubik's cube" of life from the center point of your heart. Discovering the Speed of Balance is the next step for science, business and religion, balance just being God's equation for an aesthetically pleasing integration of all elements. When there is balance, there is harmony.

Chapter 24

The Mind/Brain

While the heart is more of a *spirit,* you can view the head as more of a *force.* In the head subterminal, the mind/brain is what programs the head and activates its force. Let's talk about some of the concepts and mechanics of the mind/brain. The left side of the brain is associated with logic, reason, math, language, verbal ability, reading, writing, analysis, linear thinking or serial processing. The right side of the brain is associated with recognition of faces, patterns, symbols, rhythm, visual images, depth perception, spatial abilities, creativity, synthesis, and parallel (simultaneous) processing. While a balanced integration of both sides of the brain is ideal, in most people one side tends to operate more than the other. This is called *dominance.*

The most popular current theory of the brain is Dr. Paul MacLean's triune brain model. This theory says we actually have three brains in one: the reptilian brain, the limbic system, and the neocortex. The triune brain has developed through evolution. It began with the primitive functions of the reptilian brain. The limbic system added emotional behaviors, the sense of self, and memory that can be found in mammals. The neocortex is found only in primates and humans. It is responsible for mental activity and is much larger in humans now than it was in earlier man. According to MacLean, these three brains often strive for dominance and don't always work harmoniously together.* Many scientists think MacLean's scientific research on the triune brain will soon become outdated.

The second most popular theory of the brain is the holographic model. It was first formulated by Stanford University neurophysiologist Dr. Karl Pribram. This theory is not universally accepted because it has not yet been scientifically validated. According to this model, the brain creates a coded image. For example, it takes whatever frequency signal it sees, like this page in front of you, and translates that into a three-dimensional image. The coding is similar to what takes place in a hologram.

The holographic brain model has a *common-sense* appeal in that it also explains the structure of the universe. Michael Talbot explains in *The Holographic Universe*,

> "Our brains mathematically construct objective reality by interpreting frequencies that are ultimately projections from another dimension, a deeper order of existence that is beyond space and time: The brain is a hologram enfolded in a holographic universe."

---

* MacLean's work is cited in *Peak Learning*, by Ronald Gross (Tarcher, 1991)

As my intuition developed, I directly experienced the truth of this — my own first-hand information of the universe. Through studying the holographic head/heart relationship, I learned that the head sees disconnected segments while the heart sees the creation of the whole. Hidden within the intelligence of the heart is the power to comprehend your mind/brain in its completeness.

Scientists at the California Institute of Technology recently released information about a new discovery which revealed that human brain cells possess crystals of a highly magnetic mineral. This is the first time science has proven that magnetism exists in human cells. Animals such as whales and homing pigeons have an inborn sense of direction because of magnetic particles which orient them. At the Oak Ridge National Laboratory in Tennessee, research points to the possibility that thousands of three-dimensional images could be stored in a single magnetic crystal. According to the researchers, "By rotating the crystal slightly, a new storage opportunity is created." The holographic model is the only known process which can pack and store information that condensed. Applications based on the Oak Ridge discoveries point to a time when tremendous amounts of data may be holographically stored in a specially tailored crystal. Magnetic brain crystals are the physical counterpart of the holographic heart crystals. The recent Oak Ridge findings perfectly describe how I saw the heart crystals work.

The next step in brain research is to uncover the electrical signals that create heart-brain resonance. In his book *Vibrational Medicine*, Gerber describes scientist

Itzhak Bentov's research on heart-brain resonance. He states,

> "In Bentov's model, sonic vibrations which are created within the deep, hollow, fluid-filled ventricles of the brain by pulsations transmitted from the heart, cause a mechanical and electrical stimulation of the overlying nervous tissue."

It's interesting to note that the highest concentration of the recently discovered magnetic brain crystals were found in this same membrane enfolding the brain. It's possible, Bentov postulates, to produce "a cyclic stimulus loop of electrical activity which reverberates in a circular path through the sensory cortex.....Once the loop becomes cyclic and repetitive, the current becomes stronger."

Doc Lew Childre, in his book *Self Empowerment*, further describes this electrical circuit:

> "Your heart intuition has the capacity to engage your mind in producing subtle electrical frequencies which bring balance to the left and right hemispheres of the brain. These encoded electrical patterns regulate the brain chemistry to increase the efficiency, integrity, and effectiveness of the brain and its functions. The balance of the two brain hemispheres creates one unified electrical signal. This signal then integrates with heart and mind frequencies creating a triangulation of electrical resonance. As these three frequencies build in resonance, they form an energy field of intelligence that, for all practical purposes, translates into a third brain (which is electrical in nature, not physical). This third brain is designed to transmit and receive quantum intelligence and differentiate it down through your physical brain network for practical use in day-to-day life. As the electrical triplicity between the heart, mind and brain builds into a standing wave of resonance, it creates a unified

field of energy within the individual human mind that widens your perceptions. This electrical integration progressively activates the unused percentage of the brain potentials that science acknowledges is dormant."

At the Intui-Tech research center (a division of the Institute of HeartMath), scientific studies are being conducted to further approach the validation of heart-brain resonance. Researchers are investigating how the electrical activity associated with heart intelligence can enhance brain cells and potentially grow new ones. Experiments on how specific tonal and rhythmic patterns affect psychological patterns in people are coupled with EEG (brain) and EKG (heart) measurements. Plans include further testing of heart frequencies with EKG spectrum analysis along with EKG polygraph equipment. Institute researchers also propose to work with Superconducting Quantum Interface Device (SQUID) laboratories which use magnetic probes rather than electrodes to detect minute fluctuations in magnetic fields.

DEVELOPING THE ELECTRICAL THIRD BRAIN

The physical brain is the material vehicle for translating superconscious higher dimensional frequencies into human consciousness. The ability of the mind/brain to analyze frequencies and break them down into digits builds the conscious interface between spirit and matter. Your brain mass is an incredibly intricate network of neurons and cells that link electrical awareness to cellular physiology. Through evolution, higher mammals grew new brain cells to unfold the neocortex. Through the electrical third brain, you can grow new brain cells to receive and hold *more* higher intelligence.

You activate the higher potential of the mind/brain

by loving and caring for people and having a curiosity about "how it all works." The more you use your heart and head, together, to understand how all the parts really do function, the more of your brain potential you unfold. I studied articles on mind/brain functions, then took that information to my heart intelligence. I was curious! How could I know if I was using a larger percentage of my brain capacity? How can we as a society develop our mind/brain power and maintain balance? What kind of brain research can further intuitive development? What will be the mind/brain template of the future? I asked my heart computer to enlighten me.

I perceived that it's possible to consciously develop an electrical third brain that operates on *a software package which comes totally from the heart.* I received a picture of a paradigm of the future, when all human beings will be functioning at this capacity. I could see how conceptual understanding would become of secondary consequence. Through high-speed intuitive understanding, we will bypass the conceptual process and have direct knowing instead.

At the Institute of HeartMath, because of consistent practice in HeartMath, we've noticed that our workdays aren't cluttered with a constant need to mentally inventory each and every job detail. We've found that by focusing on our priorities — especially loving and caring for people first — the details have a way of falling into place. Many time management programs teach people how to clarify and carry out their priorities. Time management research has proven that when priorities are put first, the details become easier to manage. At the Institute, we've discovered that when you "walk your talk," productivity increases dramatically. Business runs more smoothly with a balance of heart intuition and head activity. We use intuition first, then consciously slow down the intuition when we want to use the head to access all the digits for calculation and analysis. The combination of the two brings high-speed clarity, resulting in effective action.

While the head seeks to make meaning out of everything, as intuition develops you no longer require a symbolic representation of each moment. You find that dwelling on the symbols (pictures or concepts the mind/brain presents you) slows down your direct knowing. Heart management allows you to choose between: a) real inner silence, b) intuitive analysis from your heart computer or c) digital head analysis. At the Institute, we've found that developing this flexibility heightens your *common sense* on any issue. It creates a harmonious flow where the people and the details both get taken care of. HeartMath is a system for *peace in action*.

Learning when to slow down enough to access mental programs, or when to forego such detailed analysis, is a process of finding balance. I found there's a fine line between "being in the moment" and needing to think my way through the meaning of every incoming sensory frequency signal. Since I'm sensitive to frequencies, an overload of sensory input can easily occur if I allow it. When I have a passionate love for whatever I'm doing, I bypass the need for sensory or mental signals. I intuitively get the job done without all the painstaking digits.

In my investigations, I wanted to understand the actual process the heart uses to reach intuitive decisions.

While focusing on my heart, I directed my head to break down the digits so I could study them one frame at a time and see each angle. Here's a good analogy for what I discovered: Imagine someone sitting in a forest and admiring the majesty of all the trees, then narrowing their focus to one tree limb, the beauty of its bark and the textures of the leaves. Both perspectives have value. But if you get overly focused on a tree limb, you block awareness of the whole picture. A balance of the two perspectives provides the widest understanding. The heart sees the overview, then scans the digits stored in the mind/brain to arrive at the best intuitive solution.

The information received by intuition, transmitted through your superconscious third brain, is not constricted by words nor conditioned by time. Sheets of information can pass in seconds. The Intui-Tech process eventually enables you to obtain instantaneous information on any subject. Perhaps memory will not be as important in the brain template of the future. If you can access any frequency you want, you don't need to store it in memory.

SUPERCONSCIOUS AWARENESS

The superconscious is man's link to spirit. The superconscious makes possible the necessary insight to plan and care for the needs of others and yourself. The heart intelligence would have the awareness to create "a creature with a concern for all living things," as Dr. Paul MacLean states. He describes the neocortex as the physical vehicle for this type of awareness and goes on to say, "Nature added something to the neocortex that for the first time brings a heart and a sense of compassion into the world.... As human beings, we seem to be acquiring the mental stuff of which angels are made. Perhaps it is time to take a fresh look at ourselves and try acting accordingly." The superconscious holds the electrical pattern of the human brain template, the plan of our evolution from beginning to end. Through the electrical third brain, we can develop the neocortex to its full capacity.

THE HOLOGRAPHIC BRAIN

Physicist David Bohm, a protegé of Einstein's and one of the world's most respected quantum physicists, is one of the main proponents of the holographic brain theory. He says that, "Everything in the universe is part of a continuum." As I've watched the cinematography of past, present, and future events in the holographic heart crystals — whatever the meaning of all the symbol and codes in the holographic patterns — I've seen that *spirit* is a process of continuous evolution. Reincarnation could mean living in other spheres in other universes — not just on Earth. Packed with all the information from many universes, imagine what your mind/brain would be like! What would our reality be if our brain was occupied with this information, rather than all our day-to-day problems and memories? It's possible that in the future we'll be better able to train the mind in one-pointedness and concentration, guided by heart intelligence.

I've found that the deeper and more sincere my thought, the steadier my contact and the more affinity I have with whatever I focus on. For example, if I say the word "happy" from the head, I receive information from memory of that particular thought vibration — happy. I remember times when I was happy or friends were happy. But, if I want to learn something new, I feel "happy" and sincerely set up a thought vibration from the heart. I hold that frequency and draw in knowledge that is new to me. I feel "happy" in a childlike way. Real happiness comes when you live in the heart. You're in the moment and happiness just happens.

FUTURE POTENTIALS

Life is expressed in the form of radiations, vibrations, and the weaving of energies. So, why wouldn't you be able to grow back your arm if you lost it, just like the starfish does? Lizards and earthworms also have an innate ability to grow back severed body parts. Through understanding the laws of frequencies, specialists in holographic medicine will be able to isolate radiations that animals use for regenerating physical cells.

Bees seem to have a wireless receiver (possibly carried in their antennae) that can isolate a particular radiation to lead them to their hive miles away. The homing pigeon has an innate ability and directive to fly home over great distances. It first circles around to get its bearings lined up with the earth's magnetic field. Then it flies to its destination by the most direct route possible. However, if you put a radio transmitter in the brain of the homing pigeon, it no longer can find its way — proving it's following a frequency with which the radio transmission interferes.

When you think about it, a large percentage of birds and animals have homing devices of some type. How do migrating birds know to fly back to their first home, often from thousands of miles? Why do hoards of migrating swallows return to San Juan Capistrano on almost the same day each year? We read newspaper stories of dogs and cats that have been separated from their owners, yet find their way back home over many months and hundreds of miles.

Researchers suggest that since the human nervous system is so much larger and more complex than that of smaller animals, we should be able to sense what they do, but our thoughts and emotions interfere. As humans become more *radiationally sensitive,* we will be able to learn more from the environment around us. The starfish's ability to grow back an arm would be a gift to humanity as we learn to become "atmospherically sensitive" to that particular frequency. The dolphin's sonar ability would be another frequency gift that could teach us to communicate through sonics. Using the same principle, it would also be possible to draw certain vibrations from a plant for nourishment. Or how about nourishment from a cloud? Each of these latent abilities is an isolated frequency within the spectrum of superconsciousness.

As humanity develops the power of the electrical third brain, the words we utter will automatically have more potency and electromagnetic influence. In the future, thought reading and telepathic communication will become widespread gifts, the result of simply isolating those particular frequencies. Our use of words might decrease — or at least become more economical. A balance between telepathy and word communication would seem the most efficient way to relate, involving a combination of word communication and deep listening to what another's heart and mind are trying to say.

The next step for mind/brain research is *heart/mind/ brain* research. This involves investigating the frequencies of love. What happens when people radiate more sincere feelings of love? How can we electrically measure the radiations of love? What effect does love have on brain cell regeneration? As you become more sensitive to frequencies and understand their potentials, remember that the power to do so is found in the heart. It's love and care in action that signal the Creator to release new gifts of the spirit. The power of love opens wide the door of intuition. As you practice heart management, you'll be able to understand more frequencies. However, without the foundation of heart development, you'll keep getting "out of phase." To orchestrate the mind and intuition in a harmonious interchange requires a superconscious overview. As the Doc says: "Balancing the brain hemispheres with the heart activates both its creative and linear functions, creating a joint adventure of efficiency and effectiveness."

Fifth dimensional understandings of the laws of frequencies will bring many conveniences to our world. They will be mental/emotional conveniences to start with to improve the quality of our inner lives and release stress. Mental/emotional balance is required to bring fifth dimensional frequencies into density. They only manifest when qualified by love and care. As you love and care more, you can benefit from the rewards of heart intuition long before science will be able to fully verify it.

Chapter 25

Fulfillment

I t is my hope that in your journey through this book, you've gained more understanding of what is hidden in the heart or even experienced a feeling of your own heart power. At least, maybe, you have more insight into the math of the real potency you have inside. What a magnificent force within that can facilitate change, eliminate stress, and empower us to live our lives to our fullest potential! The only secret for uncovering this power is learning to live from the heart. If I hadn't experienced, and practiced and practiced, I would never have been able to express how dynamically the heart power tools work. Still, to this day, I use the tools to sharpen my skills. The biggest difference now is it doesn't take so long to adjust my frequency and stress is easily released. I remember the adjustments I make, then if a similar stress arises I know what to do. I can see the math a bit quicker, and don't have so many mind-sets about "knowing what I know" on any subject. I still practice listening more deeply to my friends.

Life isn't perfect, but 90% of the time life's great — and the other 10% of the time life's good. I constantly remind myself to tune in with divinity, my heart intelligence. I sincerely ask questions like, "How would God look at all this?" and "What would God do?" That's the best I know to do — sincerely ask my own heart intelligence. When I want to know what the future has in store, I remember my ten-year old's simple way of looking at things. He would say, "Mom, are you in your heart? It doesn't look like it to me. You need to get back in your heart." Life in the heart is fun and adventurous. Life out of the heart is not much fun. So adjust and go back to the heart.

A quality life is not about whether you are into business, sports or education, whether you're an artist, lawyer or a blue collar worker. Simply said: *Either you are loving people or you are not loving people — in the heart or out of the heart.* Isn't that the real question to ask ourselves, especially if we hold religious beliefs? With that question in mind, it's obvious that true Christianity has never been fully practiced by society. When people journey to the "Christ within" and practice loving, that's when we'll have the chance to appreciate the heart's value and beauty. This would be the real meaning of Christianity.

There are signs of hope, even amidst the stress and distortion in the world. The iron curtain was an imposing barrier. It's come down. Yes, some ethnic groups are still squabbling over the spoils of victory. But they are also releasing the pent-up frustrations of many years and will eventually understand each other. A fence came down when two influential rival gangs saw each other as brothers instead of arch-enemies. A fence came down between science and religion with the new discoveries showing intelligent order at the beginning of creation. In the future, I do see people taking all their fences down.

Within the template of the future would be a "World Understanding" based on truth being validated by one's own heart. The foundation, the bottom line, the basis of this understanding would be "love." It will be a coming together of science and religion in the holographic heart. If you were to ask a man or woman of the future, "What is religion?", they would look at you dumbfounded and say, "Why everything!" There wouldn't be the separation of religion and education, religion and science, or — you name it. Religion wouldn't be something you just did on Sunday because you go to church. Nor would it be blindly clinging to tradition in the name of trying to keep core values alive. It would be unnatural, absurd and impractical for religion, science, math and education not to join together for the betterment of all.

"World Understanding" would be an aspect of the hidden power of the heart, an inner power that's available to everyone, a power that can change your life and create a new future for humanity. A recent Gallup poll found that while most Americans believe in God, only 10% have "transforming faith," meaning that it makes a discernible difference in their lives. This gap between belief and transforming faith can be closed by the power of heart intelligence. The Institute of HeartMath is based on the "math" of the heart — the natural laws of the head and heart that work no differently than 2+2=4. A lot of what you've read in this book you already knew in your heart. HeartMath simply organizes and interlocks your own common sense in a step-by-step way that gives you the power to act on what your heart tells you.

Practice having more efficiency with your vital energy. Practice seeing the difference between your head and your heart. Practice using the power tools in the traffic jams of life. This common-sense practice leads to self-management and self-empowerment. Then your fulfillment finds you. If you made a sincere effort to follow your heart directives every day, you'd magnetize transformation and all the fun "add-ons" in life. In his book *Self Empowerment*, the Doc states,

> "People don't have time. It's survival and ambition that are robbing the spirit of people's lives — the mind pursuits. The highest ambition and pursuit is to get heart management. Then you get the add-ons, right timing and all the conveniences. It's just streetsense. Enjoy Life."

Add-ons are those extras in life that make it fun. They are the unexpected benefits that life brings you — in ways better than you would have imagined. They are what your deepest heart would enjoy. Add-ons accumulate in proportion to your ability to go to your core heart and make peace with yourself and life. *Then life will make peace with you.* By going for a more sincere, deeper love and care for every person, you magnetize the conveniences and add-ons from life.

The revival of real family values through the heart

is quietly beginning to happen. The Gallup poll revealed that one-third of Americans now participate in a variety of small, shared-interest groups, 60% church related. "That's quite a phenomenal finding," George Gallup commented. "It's very important in our fragmented society." In such small, intimate groups, people "are finding themselves, finding others and finding God." He said that those with transforming faith were found to share a number of positive attributes, including greater tolerance, happiness, social concern and charitable leanings. According to Gallup, "We've all heard stories of people of deep faith rising above circumstances to heroic altruism. Here we have full-scale statistical evidence of it."

As you practice loving each person you meet, you will perceive at deeper levels that Earth is all one family, a global family living in one back yard. The first step of the mathematical equation for fulfillment, one that anyone can do and understand, is to just love the people. The more people in this stressful world that can build this foundation and take Step 1, the better chance humanity has.

Our forefathers founded our nation on certain truths they considered to be self-evident: That all men are created equal, that they are endowed by their Creator with certain inalienable rights. That among these are life, liberty and the pursuit of happiness. Only a foundation of loving the people can bring this to fulfillment. "World Understanding" is the hope of the future — the hope of your next moment. It is the hope of Spirit. It doesn't matter if you believe in anything, if you don't think there is life after death, or if your views about the universe are different from what I've said. The only thing that truly matters is that you love your fellow beings — the whole human race. What would be the first amendment of the constitution of the future, one that would unite religion, science, government, medicine, education? Love People! When all is said and done, what's left is the heart.

❖The Institute of HeartMath

The Institute of HeartMath is a nonprofit educational and research organization founded by Doc Lew Childre. The Institute has developed a system of energy-efficiency and self-empowerment called HeartMath™ to help people develop greater self-management, self-esteem, and reduce stress.

The Institute offers seminars based on the HeartMath system for businesses, schools, non-profit agencies, groups, the military, and families. Seminars are presented in a variety of formats, including school in-services, in-house staff development, as well as customized "learning vacations," including whitewater rafting trips, dude ranch weekends, ski trips, and other fun experiences.

- HEART EMPOWERMENT seminars are for individuals and non-profit organizations seeking creative ways to empower their personal mission while reducing stress. RECOVERY TO DISCOVERY seminars are designed for people in recovery from addictive behaviors, as well as substance abuse professionals.

- HEART SMARTS seminars are designed for educators, parents, and young people, and are based on the principles in *The How to Book of Teen Self-Discovery*. EMPOWERING THE CHILD is designed for students, parents and educators.

- EMPOWERING THE HEART OF BUSINESS seminars and training programs are designed to help businesses increase care and efficiency based on the techniques outlined in the book, *Self Empowerment: The Heart Approach to Stress Management; Common Sense Strategies,* by Doc Lew Childre.

For more information on seminars and
training programs, contact:

THE INSTITUTE OF HEARTMATH
P.O. Box 1463 • Boulder Creek, CA 95006
408-338-6803 • Fax 408-338-9861

SELF EMPOWERMENT:
The Heart Approach to Stress
Management; Common Sense
Strategies
by Doc Lew Childre

In this practical and timely
book, Doc Lew Childre offers effective common sense strategies
that can empower you to relieve
the stress of today's personal, family, social and business problems.
Topics include:

- Intui-Technology™—the science of intuitive
  development
- The advantages of the men's and women's movements
- Intuitive levels of time management
- How to balance your inner female/male nature
- Techniques to eliminate relationship drains
- How to care without stress from overcare
- The family concept—the business trend for efficiency
  and effectiveness
- Sexual harassment—the intelligence beyond it
- Strategies for finally being your true self
- Accessing the power of your "heart intuition"

"The message is a strong one and the methodology can
be understood and adopted by many. The potential
release of positive energy is formidable."
J. Tracy O'Rourke, Chairman and CEO, Varian Associates

"Now here's the book for people who are really serious
about improving their lives. A refreshingly hopeful
and positive vision of the world [that] can transform
the workplace, the schoolroom, the home, and all social
situations."
Dr. Joyce Chumbley, Educational consultant

$13.95 (paper); $22.95 (cloth) plus shipping and handling

HEART ZONES:
A Musical Solution for Stress
by Doc Lew Childre

"Music is like a food for the psyche. Unbalanced food leads to negative feedback in your system, whether it be physical food or food for the psyche (music, impressions, color, thoughts, etc.)," according to Doc Lew Childre, composer of *Heart Zones*. Both young people and adults benefit from the right "vitamin-charged food."

"The Doc" designed *Heart Zones* to prevent stress and release people's accumulated stress build-up, while creating an enhanced learning or working environment. It's like a fun tonic for your mental and emotional nature.

"I enjoyed **Heart Zones**. Very beneficial for stress management."
  David J. Fletcher, M.D., Occupational and Preventive Medicine, Midwest Occupational Health Associates

"**Heart Zones** is excellent. I use Heart Zones as an adjunct to psychotherapy. I've seen immediate results with many patients, including reduced anxiety and more sustained focus during therapy sessions."
  Marshall Gilula, M.D., Psychiatrist

"It really really works. When I need to relax, I put on cut four. When I need to get going in the morning with a positive attitude, it's cut one. When it's time to write or get something done in a hurry, cut three brings focus and speed. The effects are discreet and effective and the instrumentation and presentation are right on the mark. [Heart Zones] is responsible for my high productivity!"
  Scott Schuster, Editorial Director, Executive Programs, national magazine

Cassette $9.95 • Compact disc $15.98 plus shipping and handling

THE HOW TO BOOK OF TEEN SELF DISCOVERY:
Helping Teens Find Balance, Security and Esteem
by Doc Lew Childre

Parents, educators, and teens alike will enjoy this new edition of Doc's popular first book, *Heart Smarts: Teenage Guide for the Puzzle of Life*, which is approved as a textbook by the State of California. Here's what reviewers had to say about the first edition.

"Very powerful. It assumes that teenagers *can* develop self-esteem and self-control, and that they *want* to. Then it shows them how."
Religion Teacher's Journal

"An excellent job of introducing teenagers to their feelings—and to healthy self-esteem. I applaud Doc Childre for his sensitivity to the needs of young people and for this most excellent tool for teenagers, adults and teachers. I recommend it highly."
Emmett E. Miller, M.D.
California Task Force to Promote Self-Esteem and Personal and Social Responsiblity

"Helps teens learn how to deal with the resentments, judgments and boredom that keep them unfulfilled. Learning to care for others; to practice appreciation for people, places and things, and to not judge other people or themselves, are some of the 'power tools' that Childre advocates to build the real security and self-esteem teenagers are looking for."
College Preview: A Guide for College & Career Bound Students

$8.95 plus shipping and handling

ORDERING INFORMATION

To order books, tapes, and compact discs, please send check, money order or credit card information to:

Planetary Publications
P.O. Box 66 • 14700 West Park Ave.
Boulder Creek, California, 95006
408-338-2161 / 800-372-3100 • Fax 408-338-9861

- Please include shipping and handling costs: $2.50 for first item, $1.00 each additional item (book rate).
- For UPS delivery, add $1.00 to total shipping and handling costs. (Foreign residents should double the shipping and handling rates.)
- California residents include 7.25% sales tax.
- Visa, Mastercard, and American Express accepted. Please include expiration date, card number and full name on card.
- For convenience, place your order using our toll-free number — 800-372-3100, 24 hours a day, 7 days a week, or fax us your order at 408-338-9861.

INDEX